ALSO BY DON GABOR

SPEAKING YOUR MIND IN 101 DIFFICULT SITUATIONS

Don Gabor

A FIRESIDE BOOK
A Stonesong Press Book
Published by Simon & Schuster
New York   London   Toronto   Sydney   Tokyo   Singapore

FIRESIDE
Simon & Schuster Building
Rockefeller Center
1230 Avenue of the Americas
New York, New York 10020

Manufactured in the United States of America

1   3   5   7   9   10   8   6   4   2

Library of Congress Cataloging-in-Publication Data

Gabor, Don.
Speaking your mind in 101 difficult situations / Don Gabor.
p.   cm
"A Stonesong Press book."
1. Interpersonal communication.   2. Tact.   I. Title.   II. Title:
Speaking your mind in one-hundred-and-one difficult situations.
BF637.C45G335   1994
158'.2—dc20   93–41345
                                                                  CIP

ISBN: 0-671-79505-8

Dedication
and Acknowledgments

This book is dedicated to my wife, Eileen; to my parents, Trude and Fred; and to my sister and her husband, Ellen and John Newport. I also dedicate this book to everyone who has ever said the wrong thing—and wished they hadn't.

I want to offer my special thanks to Eileen Cowell for her wise words, sharp editorial pencil, and loving patience during this project. I want to thank my friends for sharing their personal experiences and suggestions. I also want to express my gratitude to Sheree Bykofsky and Paul Fargis at The Stonesong Press, and Ed Walters at Simon & Schuster/Fireside for their inspiration and guidance in the creation and writing of this book. Finally, I want to thank my faithful office cat, Sophie, for sitting on my computer monitor and keeping me company during the many months it took me to complete this book.

Contents

PART III
TACTFUL TALK IN YOUR PERSONAL RELATIONSHIPS

Introduction

A husband tells his wife that her new dress is okay but would look better on her if she lost fifteen pounds. She leaves the room in tears. He yells, *"I said the dress looks okay—what's your problem?"*

A woman informs a coworker that his breath smells like a dead fish. He suddenly turns beet red and acts distant and cold. She protests, *"I was just kidding!"*

Do you often say the wrong thing, offend others, and end your conversations on a sour note? Do you find yourself in difficult situations, but you don't know what to say or how to say it? Do you wonder why some people make friends when they talk, but all you end up with is cold and unfriendly stares?

HOW TO USE THIS BOOK

Speaking Your Mind in 101 Difficult Situations can help. In "Part I: Mastering the Art of Tact," you will learn seven vital communications strategies that can help you build your confidence in your ability to say what you need to say in any difficult conversation. You will also learn how to improve your listening skills, stay calm in difficult conversations, become an assertive communicator, and cope with difficult people.

In "Part II: Tactful Talk in the Workplace and Business World," you'll learn *what to say* in 41 difficult situations with your boss, coworkers, subordinates, and business associates. In "Part III: Tactful Talk in Your Personal Relationships," you'll learn *what to say* in 60 difficult situations with your friends, sweetheart, spouse, children, family members, and relatives. Each of the

101 entries includes several examples that you can adapt to your specific situation.

The strategies and skills presented in Part I are referred to throughout the rest of the book. Review them along with any of the specific examples that correspond to your own situation. That way you'll have the confidence and know-how to speak your mind in any conversation.

THIS BOOK CAN HELP YOU IN MANY WAYS

This book can help you advance your career and improve the quality of your life in the workplace. If you are a manager, this book can help you communicate more effectively with your staff. If you are single, this book can help you find a compatible mate. Parents, this book can guide you to help your kids to do better in school and increase harmony in your family. All of these benefits come about by improving your ability to communicate with tact. So turn this page and let's begin!

PART I

MASTERING THE ART OF TACT

CHAPTER 1

Seven Strategies for T-A-C-T-F-U-L Conversations

Oh, no! Another tough personal situation in which putting your foot in your mouth seems like a foregone conclusion. Well, you don't have to be a communication klutz anymore—that is, if you use the following seven strategies for tactful conversations. But first . . .

WHAT IS TACT?

Tact is the ability to recognize the delicacy of a situation and then to say the most considerate or most appropriate thing. Tact requires a sensitivity to others, combined with the skill to speak assertively at any given time without giving offense. It is the talent for managing difficult circumstances or people. Tact requires ingenuity and the ability to know what will make a person feel better after talking to you.

If you're worried about your communication skills, this may sound like a difficult challenge. Fortunately there is an easy way to learn the basic elements of tact.

T-A-C-T-F-U-L

Each letter in the word *T-A-C-T-F-U-L* stands for one of seven strategies that will help you say the right thing in any sticky conversation!

T = Think before you speak
A = Apologize quickly when you blunder
C = Converse, don't compete
T = Time your comments
F = Focus on behavior—not on personality
U = Uncover hidden feelings
L = Listen for feedback

T = Think Before You Speak

T in the word *T-A-C-T-F-U-L* stands for "Think before you speak." The best way to prevent a verbal blunder is not to say it in the first place. Avoid a tactless comment by thinking about what you want to say and how you want to say it *before* you say it. Many quick-tongued people don't realize the negative impact their sharp words can have on others. Therefore, rather than "shooting from the lip" and slamming others with your brutal honesty, take a deep breath and ask yourself:

"How would I feel if someone said this to me?"

"What do I want my words to accomplish?"

"What response would I like to hear?"

"Are my expectations reasonable?"

"For whose benefit am I saying this?"

"How will the other person feel after I speak?"

"Are my comments hurtful or helpful?"

In many instances, if you take a moment to put yourself in the other person's shoes, you can avoid saying something tactless. Use your own feelings as a yardstick. If you feel even mildly offended by what you are going to say, then others probably will too. In this case, don't say anything until you can rephrase your comment in a more thoughtful way.

A — *Apologize Quickly When You Blunder*

A in the word **T-A-C-T-F-U-L** stands for "Apologize quickly when you blunder." A case in point: When Jane is introduced to a coworker's spouse, she blurts out, *"Ann, I thought your husband was so much younger."* After noticing the couple's embarrassed glances and thin smiles, Jane realizes she has made a very tactless comment. She quickly apologizes and then changes the subject.

Everyone makes a verbal blunder from time to time. The trick is to recognize that you have put your foot in your mouth and then take it out immediately. Tuning in to the other person's verbal and nonverbal reactions will tell you if an apology is necessary. If you do say the wrong thing:

- Apologize immediately
- Acknowledge your mistake
- Avoid elaborate excuses because you'll probably just dig yourself into a deeper hole
- Repeat your apology with a touch of humility
- Change the topic to an upbeat subject

Jane can minimize the damage from her rude comment by saying something like:

"I'm sorry! Ann, it's just that the way you talk about your 'youthful' husband, I just assumed that he was barely out of his twenties and not such a distinguished gentleman! By the way, I understand you two just returned from a vacation in Europe and I'd love to hear all about it. Where exactly did you go?"

C = *Converse, Don't Compete*

C in the word **T-A-C-T-F-U-L** stands for "Converse, don't compete." Do you approach conversations as a competition in which there is a winner and a loser? Is it your aim to fascinate people with your knowledge and verbal skill by punching holes in their opinions, arguing over details, or correcting their mistakes? If you adopt an aggressive, "talk to win" conversational style, then you'll certainly impress people, but in the wrong way. Competitive talkers tend to be tactless and boring because they see conversations as a debate rather than a mutual exchange of information, ideas, opinions, and feelings.

To communicate tactfully, replace a competitive approach with a less aggressive and more casual conversational style. Then, when you express your views, people will be more inclined to listen without taking offense at an opinion that may differ from their own.

T = Time Your Comments

T in the word ***T-A-C-T-F-U-L*** stands for "Time your comments." Before you lay your conversational cards on the table, be sure the person to whom you wish to present your viewpoint is ready to listen. If you spout off too early or too late, you'll be wasting your breath and your opportunity to get your point across. How do you know when the time is right? "Perfect" moments rarely occur, but some are definitely better or worse than others. If at all possible, avoid discussing sensitive or personal topics:

- In public places or in the company of your friends or co-workers
- The minute the other person arrives home from work
- First thing in the morning
- When you or the other person are upset
- When outside distractions such as television, kids, or telephone calls make it impossible to talk without interruption
- Right before, during, or after you have sex

Your conversational timing will improve if you:

- Agree upon a time to talk
- Get right to the point
- Do not insist upon an immediate response or agreement
- Show a willingness to listen

To emphasize your awareness of timing in a conversation and to give the other person an opportunity to consider your problem, feelings, request, or point of view carefully, you can say,

"I'm not asking for a decision or response right now, but please think about what I've said. We can talk about it again

in a few minutes, later today, tomorrow, or whenever it is a good time for you."

F = Focus on Behavior—Not on Personality

F in the word **T-A-C-T-F-U-L** stands for "Focus on behavior—not on personality." For example, do you have a difficult friend who aggravates you? Some people just love to complain, dwell on the negative, procrastinate, and make excuses. However, when a friend's actions threaten your relationship, you have the right to speak up. The tactful approach is to identify the annoying behavior rather than focus on changing his or her personality. Remember, it is much easier for a person to change specific, identifiable actions than it is to alter his or her entire character.

For instance, perhaps you have a "perfectionist" friend, who has the aggravating habit of always correcting grammatical errors or minor details of a story as you or others speak. Rather than be inhibited, embarrassed, and angered by your friend's compulsive need to be correct—you won't be able to change that—do something about the behavior. The next time your friend contradicts or corrects you, quietly take him aside and say something like:

"John, can I talk to you privately for a moment? I know that you are just trying to help, but when you constantly correct or contradict me as I speak, it's rude and makes me look foolish. It really makes me feel uncomfortable and embarrasses everyone else too. Would it be too much to ask you just to let the little, inconsequential details go by instead of calling them to everyone's attention?"

If your friend says that he was just trying to help get the facts straight, then say:

"Let me explain it this way. When you correct someone else in public—even if you are right—it makes you look like a person who is trying to make yourself look good at some other poor dummy's expense. If you feel compelled to set

the record straight, you can show a lot more tact by men-
tioning it to the person in private."

U = Uncover Hidden Feelings

U in the word *T-A-C-T-F-U-L* stands for "Uncover hidden feelings." Saying difficult things tactfully is more likely if you first
attempt to uncover and understand the other person's feelings.
For example, if your worried parent implies that your decision
to make a planned investment is irresponsible, *don't say:*

"Why don't you mind your own business and stop treating
me like a kid—it's my money and I'll do with it as I want!"

This typical defensive and childish response does little to inspire
your parent's confidence in you. Find out if any other hidden
feelings lurk behind the critical comment. In this situation perhaps your parent wants to prevent you from making a costly
mistake similar to one he made in the past. Or maybe he feels
insecure about his own financial future and is not sure how to
bring the subject up in a direct manner. Once you uncover the
real reasons and needs behind critical comments or undesirable
behavior, you can tailor a tactful response to address the real
issues. You might say:

"Dad, I appreciate your concern about my investments, but
it sounds like you are worried about something else too. Is
there something going on that you want to talk to me
about?"

L = Listen for Feedback

L in the word *T-A-C-T-F-U-L* stands for "Listen for feedback."
Poor listening skills frequently lead to tactless comments. Criticism or indiscreet remarks often stem from a desire to dominate the conversation without considering what the other
person has to say. However, when you carefully listen for feedback and reactions to your comments, you will know if your
conversational partner is listening to you and understands your

viewpoint and feelings. You'll also learn what issues he or she is sensitive to and willing to discuss and whether or not he or she feels receptive to your opinions. The next chapter presents ten specific ways to boost your listening skills and as a result improve your ability to communicate with tact.

Be T-A-C-T-F-U-L All the Time

Use these **T-A-C-T-F-U-L** strategies whenever you talk to people—even when you are not in difficult or stressful conversations. Then when you are faced with a pressured situation, you will have had some practice with the techniques.

DOS AND DON'TS TO ACCOMPANY
T-A-C-T-F-U-L STRATEGIES

Do be direct, courteous, and calm.
Don't be rude or pushy.
Do spare others your unsolicited advice.
Don't be patronizing, superior, or sarcastic.
Do acknowledge that what works for you may not work for others.
Don't make personal attacks or insinuations.
Do say main points first, then offer more details if necessary.
Don't expect others to follow your advice or always agree with you.
Do listen for hidden feelings.
Don't suggest changes that a person cannot easily make.

CHAPTER 2

Ten Ways to Boost Your Listening Skills

"A good listener is not *someone who has to be checked every now and then by the speaker to see if he or she is awake."*
—JUDITH MARTIN, also known as MISS MANNERS

How do you feel when a person shows interest and enthusiasm in what you say? Flattered, of course, that someone thinks you've got something to say! An interested listener makes you feel appreciated, confident, and good about yourself. Most people, on the other hand, see poor listeners as rude individuals who appear disinterested and unwilling to acknowledge other people's opinions, feelings, and experiences. Poor listening skills lead to tactless remarks, which can swiftly lead to personal and business conflicts. The choice is up to you—to listen or not to listen. So how exactly do you show someone you are listening?

Here are ten easy ways to boost your ability to listen effectively:

1. Eliminate external and internal distractions
2. Encourage the other person to speak first
3. Use and observe body language
4. Avoid unnecessary interruptions
5. Listen for key words
6. Use reflective listening

7. Clarify implied statements
8. Identify and focus on main points
9. Silently review and order main points and draw your conclusions
10. Acknowledge the speaker's viewpoint

Let's look at each of these in more detail.

ELIMINATE EXTERNAL AND INTERNAL DISTRACTIONS

External and internal distractions are the major factors that interfere with listening. Therefore the first way to improve your listening ability is to eliminate as many distractions as possible. It is crucial to give people your complete attention so that you can focus on their body language, what they say, what they *don't* say, and what feelings and meanings their words imply.

External distractions include a blaring television or radio, screaming kids, ringing telephones, playing with a pencil, doodling, or preparing dinner. Here are some ways to say that you want to eliminate external distractions:

"I'm going to shut off the television (radio, stereo, etc.) while we discuss this problem, because we both need to listen carefully to what is being said."

"I'll unplug the phone while we talk so we're not interrupted."

"I've put the Do Not Disturb sign on my door so we can talk without interruption. I really want to hear what you have to say."

Internal distractions, while less obvious, are equally detrimental to listening. Internal distractions include daydreaming, worrying, tuning out, excessive note-taking, focusing only on facts, or mentally debating with the speaker. Here are some ways to say that you want to eliminate internal distractions:

"I've got a lot of things on my mind, but I'm going to forget about them for the moment while we talk. I want to listen and make sure I understand what you are saying."

"I'm not going to worry about finding an immediate solution to this problem. I just want to listen and make sure I know how you are feeling about it."

"While I have my own opinions of why we are having this problem, I'm going to put my views aside for the time being and listen to what you have to say. I want to get a clear idea of where you stand on this issue."

ASK THE OTHER PERSON TO SPEAK FIRST

There are three reasons to encourage other people to present their views before you do. First, listening shows good etiquette and a desire to consider another person's viewpoint objectively. This makes the speaker feel that you value his or her opinions, thus building rapport and receptivity.

Second, encouraging the other person to talk reduces competition in the conversation. Your listening creates an open atmosphere conducive to a mutual exchange of views. Without the competitive element to worry them, speakers can focus on the main ideas rather than quibble over inconsistencies.

Third, asking the other person to share his or her views lets you identify areas of agreement before you present your views. Once you have established receptivity by listening, your ability to persuade increases. Here are some ways to encourage the other person to talk first:

"I'm very much interested in your opinion about . . ."

"I'd like to hear your insights about . . ."

"I'd first like to know how you feel about the situation. Then I'll tell you how I see it from my perspective."

"We both have a lot to say, so why don't you begin with how you see the problem."

USE AND OBSERVE BODY LANGUAGE

Did you know your body language speaks before you do and sends messages of interest or boredom in a conversation? Imagine how good you'd feel about yourself if someone with whom you were talking was wide-eyed, leaning forward, smiling and responding to your words with enthusiasm and excitement? In contrast, do you remember how awkward and uncomfortable you felt when you were in a conversation with someone who was leaning back in his chair, yawning, frowning, crossing his arms, staring at the ground, and saying little or nothing?

It is not hard to understand why a listener's closed or disinterested body language makes the speaker feel self-conscious and less willing to open up. On the other hand, open or interested body language shows a receptive listener who wants to understand, and thus encourages the person to talk. When you're trying to communicate with someone, *show* them that you're listening.

Open body language includes:

- Smiling casually
- Uncrossing your arms
- Keeping your hands away from your face
- Leaning forward slightly
- Frequent eye contact
- Nodding your head

Closed body language is just the opposite: for example, crossed arms, leaning back in your chair, infrequent eye contact, and so on.

Look at the Other Person's Body Language for Clues

Awareness of a speaker's body language also enhances your listening abilities. By focusing your attention on *how* something is said as well as on *what* is said, you zero in on the speaker's sensitive areas, concerns, and hidden feelings. This "listening between the lines" helps prevent tactless comments, which can offend or lead to an argument.

AVOID UNNECESSARY INTERRUPTIONS

Good listeners do not interrupt a speaker to make trivial points, petty corrections, abrupt changes of topic, or to complete an unfinished sentence. Frequent interruptions indicate poor listening skills, an aggressive attitude, lousy manners, and for the most part little communication.

Two exceptions to the rule of avoiding interruptions:

First, the Ping-Pong effect of a lively conversation contains many timely interruptions with relevant questions, comments, or repartee that advance the discussion toward its conclusion.

Second, there are situations when you will need to interrupt a speaker because you missed an important fact, do not understand a concept, or you need clarification on a point that the speaker has made. When you find yourself in this situation, wait for the other person's *briefest* pause and then quickly say:

"Sorry to interrupt you, but I missed the spelling of your last name. Could you give it to me again, please, before you go on?"

"I want to stop you right here because you're talking way over my head. I'm afraid I don't understand any of the technical details of the computer that you are showing me."

"Excuse me, but I thought I heard you say . . . and I just want to make sure that I heard correctly before you continue."

LISTEN FOR KEY WORDS

Conversations are made up of many hundreds of words, some more important than others. Key words in a conversation are the ones that paint mental pictures. These key words convey information and also show interest and emotions. Think of a key word as the tip of an iceberg. Much more information about that topic lies just below the surface waiting to be talked about.

Key words are clues to topics that people enjoy talking about or information they want you to know. Most people consciously and unconsciously sprinkle key words throughout their conversation, but it is up to the good listener to pick them out and refer to them through questions or comments. Here are some statements in which the key words are highlighted. They are followed by a question or related experience based on one or more of the key words.

If someone says:

> *"I went to Hawaii on vacation about five years ago. That was before I moved to New York, went back to school to get my business degree, and opened a restaurant."*

You can ask a question based on one or two key words:

> *"What made you decide to go into the restaurant business?"*

If someone says:

> *"I live in a little house with a small backyard where I grow vegetables and where my cats, Sophie and Toby, chase squirrels."*

You can share a related experience based on the key words:

> *"I have two cats too! Mine love to chase the birds on the balcony."*

Key Words Reveal Personal Information

Some key words reveal trust and a desire to discuss a sensitive topic. When you hear a key word that refers to a personal issue, it tells you that this subject is probably open for discussion.
  If someone says:

> *"I've been single for about a year and I'm starting to date again, but I'm not seeing anyone special."*

You can reveal your marital status by referring to key words:

> *"I was married once, too, but I've been dating on and off for about the last two years.*

If someone says:

"I'm a little nervous about telling my parents about my new job. I know my mom and dad are going to be upset when I tell them I'm moving away."

You can share a related experience by referring to key words:

"I know what you mean about being nervous. My parents were concerned when I told them I was moving to New York."

Key Words Help You Know What to Say Next

By identifying key words in a conversation you can decide how to respond. By simply repeating the key word in a question or statement, you can show your conversational partner that you are interested or concerned. Here are some ways to refer to key words:

"I heard you mention earlier that you enjoyed playing (key word) *in your spare time. That's one of my hobbies too."*

"When you said you are working in the field of (key word), *I was wondering how you got into that profession."*

"You said you're from (key word). *I've never been there. What is it like?"*

USE REFLECTIVE LISTENING

Reflective listening is an important communication skill in which you rephrase what you've heard someone say. It demonstrates that you have been listening and understand what the speaker has told you. However, reflective listening is not parroting the person word for word. Instead it is using your own words to summarize the other person's main points. Here are some examples of statements or questions that utilize reflective listening skills:

"You said you live in a house by the beach? I bet the sunsets must be beautiful!"

"When you mentioned a few minutes ago that you are taking an oil-painting class at the local college, it made me wonder if I could find the time to pursue a hobby. I've always thought it would be fun to learn how to paint with oils."

"If I understand you correctly, you feel left out when you don't get to go to the movies on Friday night with your friends. Is that right?"

"I want to make sure that I understand your position. It's your opinion that . . ."

"I think I understand what you want, but let me summarize what you've said, and then you tell me if I've interpreted your comments correctly."

The Benefits of Reflective Listening

The rewards of using reflective listening skills include:

- Building rapport and receptivity
- Making the other person feel important
- Allowing you to focus on the essential elements of the conversation
- Helping correct misconceptions and false assumptions quickly
- Speaking more spontaneously
- Keeping the conversation going

CLARIFY IMPLIED STATEMENTS

Many people are afraid to state their thoughts and feelings directly. Instead they suggest their true opinions and true feelings through implied statements or questions. They may also have hidden assumptions or goals that remain unstated with the hope that the listener will "get the message" without having to be told in so many words. Implied statements confuse communication because the poor listener often misinterprets the speaker's meaning or purpose, which can lead to verbal blunders or arguments.

The first step in overcoming this communication problem is to listen carefully for a speaker's "loaded" statements or questions, which imply much more than they actually say. A speaker's tone of voice and the words he or she emphasizes reveal a great deal. Here are some examples in which the "loaded" words are highlighted. They are followed by information-seeking questions, which encourage the speaker to be more specific.

If someone says:

"*I'm not all that crazy about it.*"

You can ask:

"*Tell me exactly, what don't you like about it?*"

If someone says:

"*It ought to be pretty clear what I think about that great idea of yours.*"

You can say:

"*I have no idea what you think of my idea. Do you like it or not?*"

If someone says:

"*You know what I'm trying to say.*"

You can respond:

"*No, I don't. Please tell me exactly what you mean.*"

If someone says:

"*After all I've done for you, I expected more than this.*"

You can ask:

"What exactly did you expect?"

Asking Questions Clarifies Meaning

Asking the speaker to clarify implied statements greatly decreases your chances of making a verbal blunder and helps uncover hidden sensitivities. First ask yourself, *"What is he **not** saying?"* and then ask the other person directly:

"Although you didn't say so directly, you seem to be suggesting that. . . . Is that what you mean?"

"I'm not exactly sure what you mean by. . . . Could you explain it to me with a little more detail and give me some examples?"

"From what you are saying, I'm getting the distinct impression that you feel . . . , but I'm not sure that's what you mean. Is my impression right or wrong?"

"Forgive me, but when you say you'll 'more or less finish' painting my kitchen by Friday, what exactly do you mean?"

"I'm not really sure what you mean when you say that you 'expected more' from me. Could you give me a few examples of how I disappointed you."

"From what you've said, I presume you mean. . . . Is that correct?"

IDENTIFY AND FOCUS ON MAIN POINTS

While it may be tempting to debate the finer details of an issue, identifying and focusing on a speaker's main points helps you to see the "big picture" from his or her point of view. When you avoid focusing on trivial facts, you don't waste time and make false assumptions because you missed important points and main ideas.

A good listener traces the development of the speaker's main ideas and then makes an effort to predict where these important points are leading. This listening skill helps you stay actively involved in the conversation and determines how effectively you and the other person are communicating. If you consistently identify, follow, and anticipate the other person's main ideas and conclusions correctly, then you are listening and communicating skillfully.

If, however, you find that you are bogged down in details, missing main points, making false assumptions, and jumping to conclusions, then go back and see where your understanding of the speaker's main points went astray. Here are ways to question or make a statement about a speaker's main point:

"What exactly is your point?"

"I'm not sure I understand your main point."

"If I understand you correctly, your main point is. . . ."

"Can you please just tell me the bottom line."

SILENTLY REVIEW AND ORDER MAIN POINTS
AND DRAW YOUR CONCLUSIONS

There comes a time in most conversations where you can steal a few moments to mentally review and order the main points made by the other person. Order the main points starting with what you believe the speaker considers the most important. This eliminates irrelevant details and allows you to focus on and remember the speaker's main points and big ideas.

Silently reviewing and ordering main points also provides an opportunity to ask follow-up questions. Referring to incomplete or ambiguous points shows the speaker that you are listening and trying hard to understand his or her ideas fully. If you are not sure of the priority of the main points or ideas in a conversation, then ask,

"Out of the several excellent points you've brought out in our discussion, which ones are the three most important?"

"From all the ideas you've come up with, which one do you want me to focus on the most?"

"Of all the material we talked about today, what two ideas did you find the most useful?"

Once you've mentally reviewed and ordered the main points, rephrase what you believe to be the speaker's conclusion. Rephrasing and summary statements may sound like one of the following:

"Let me see if I understand your conclusion correctly. You believe that . . ."

"In the final analysis you've decided to. . . ."

"From what you've said, you've decided to. . . ."

"I'm not sure I see what you're driving at. Will you tell me please?"

"What conclusions should I draw from what you have said?"

"This means that you have concluded. . . ."

"Now that all is said and done, is it correct to say that you want . . . ?"

"From what you've said, I understand that your bottom line is. . . ."

"If we take care of those final details, then can I assume that we have a deal?"

When you rephrase and summarize what you've heard, the other person's response may surprise you. It can range from, ***"That's not what I meant at all,"*** to ***"Not quite. Let me clarify a point for you,"*** to ***"That's exactly right!"*** If you've understood correctly, you proceed to the next step in the conversation. If not, go back and clarify the point you've misunderstood.

ACKNOWLEDGE THE SPEAKER'S VIEWPOINT

You can miss many opportunities to build rapport if you fail to acknowledge the other person's viewpoint. Accept your conversational partner's right to his or her opinions, conclusions, and feelings—even though they may differ from yours. To acknowledge another point of view, you can say something like:

"Now I understand that you feel . . ."

"I now know what you mean when you say . . ."

"Now that I understand your circumstances, I see why you feel . . ."

"Before you told me about . . . I didn't understand, but now I can see it from your perspective."

"Your points make perfect sense, even though I see the situation differently."

The message here is that you listened, you now understand, and while you may not agree, you respect the other person's viewpoint. Without acknowledgment there is little hope for establishing receptivity or rapport. In addition, skillful listening builds the speaker's self-esteem and makes him or her more open to outside arguments. Finally, listening signals approval and encourages people to reach a mutual agreement.

LISTENING IS A LEARNED SKILL THAT IMPROVES WITH PRACTICE

Listening effectively is a vital link in the communication chain. Try to exercise these ten listening skills with everyone you talk to, even during informal or brief conversations. Then, when you find yourself in a more challenging or difficult conversation, you will have the confidence to use your listening skills for the maximum results.

CHAPTER 3

Staying Calm in Difficult Conversations

How do you react in difficult or stressful conversations? Are you poised and confident when presenting a proposal to your boss, giving a speech, or interviewing for a job? Do you remain cool under fire if an irritated coworker, angry lover, or a dominating family member verbally attacks you? If you're like most people, difficult conversations make you feel nervous. Your heart pounds, your mouth gets dry, there are butterflies in your stomach, and you do not communicate well!

People are nervous and lack confidence in difficult conversations because they are afraid of sounding ridiculous, saying the wrong thing, angering the other person, or losing something important—like their respect, job, or lover! Fear undermines your confidence only if you let it, because you *can* control nervousness and stay calm in difficult conversations. Five basic communication techniques can help you increase your confidence, verbal effectiveness, and personal power. They are: (1) relaxing; (2) visualizing; (3) affirming; (4) scripting; and (5) practicing.

TECHNIQUE #1: RELAX YOUR MUSCLES TO CALM YOUR MIND

Studies show that the more physically relaxed you are, the better your concentration and mental focus are. This can make it much easier to deal with a difficult conversation. Use the following exercises to help relax the muscles in your shoulders, neck, face, and back while reducing stress, tension, and anxiety.

Exercise #1: Tell Yourself to Relax

This is a simple, yet effective way to relax your muscles at home, at work, while you are walking, driving, or anywhere else. Remind yourself throughout your day to:

"Relax your back."
"Unclench your fists."
"Loosen your jaw."

Focus on keeping those muscles relaxed as you walk, sit, and go about your daily activities by saying:

"My shoulders are relaxed."
"My neck is relaxed."
"My back is relaxed."
"My jaw is relaxed."

As soon as you notice the tension returning to those areas of your body, remind yourself to relax again.

Exercise #2: Deep Breathing

You can use this exercise at home, in your office, or on a park bench:

- Sit in a chair and place your feet flat on the floor.
- Press your palms and fingers together with a moderate amount of pressure, like in an isotonic exercise.
- Point your fingers upward and your elbows gently outward away from your body.
- Inhale deeply and slowly through your nose while contracting the muscles in the pit of your stomach. Continue to push your hands together.
- Exhale gently through your mouth while saying the word **Hissssssss.** Picture an inflated balloon with its air slowly escaping.

• Relax your hands, elbows, and the muscles in your shoulders, face, neck, and back.

Repeat this exercise several times, whenever you feel anxious or before you enter a stressful situation.

Exercise #3: Counting Backward

This is a relaxation exercise you can do at home, or with your office door closed:

• Lie with your back flat on the floor and your legs uncrossed. Place your hands slightly below your navel.
• Inhale and exhale gently and slowly as you begin counting backward from ten to one.
• As you say each number, relax the muscles at the top of your head, your eyebrows, mouth, neck, shoulders, chest, and back. Feel the tension in your muscles leaving your body through your fingertips.
• Repeat the counting exercise, this time beginning with the muscles in your toes, feet, calves, legs, and lower back.

TECHNIQUE #2: VISUALIZE SUCCESSFUL OUTCOMES TO BUILD CONFIDENCE

Visualization is an ancient process of using your mind's eye to create a mental picture of something that you would like to achieve, such as resolving a misunderstanding between you and a friend. When your imagination captures the sensations of achieving a particular goal before you make an actual attempt, you will feel more confident that a successful outcome is possible. Visualizing does not control other people's behavior, but rather helps you dissolve fears and doubts about what you can achieve.

Exercise #1: Visualize Your Goals As If They Already Exist

The power of visualization rests in your ability to evoke optimistic thoughts and feelings associated with a specific goal as if it is already happening. For example, let's say your specific goal is to remain calm while presenting a proposal to your high-strung and critical boss. Visualize the meeting this way:

- Find a place where you can relax and close your eyes.
- Use your imagination to picture yourself walking into your boss's office with poise and composure. Use your sense of sight, smell, touch, taste, and hearing to enhance your visualization. Focus on all the details that you see, hear, smell, and touch in the office. Be sure to include your boss in the visualization.
- In your mind's eye, see and hear yourself confidently discussing the proposal with your boss, and see his or her skeptical response.
- See yourself responding to your boss's questions and doubt with grace and clarity. Concentrate on your confidence as you and your boss discuss your proposal.
- Remember to visualize the situation as though it were happening right now.
- When your fears and doubts creep into your visualization, don't worry or try to suppress them. Let them play out for a short time like a bad soap opera on television. Then eliminate your fears and doubts from your visualization by switching off the television set.
- Refocus your visualization so that your meeting ends successfully and see your boss smiling, nodding, and accepting your proposal.
- Repeat your visualization frequently until you achieve your goal.

ANOTHER BENEFIT OF VISUALIZATION

In addition to building confidence, visualizing a specific goal and situation can reveal certain weaknesses or flaws in your approach that you may not have considered, thus providing you with an opportunity to address them before the "real" presentation.

Exercise #2: Clearing Your Mind of Doubts and Fears

Try this visualization exercise the next time fears and doubts creep into your thoughts and make you feel tense:

- Imagine yourself standing in a field beside a wooden box with its top open. A pile of rocks with words written on them sits beside the box.
- The words on the rocks name the fears, doubts, and reasons that prevent you from achieving your goals. For example, one might say that you're bored with your present job but you feel that you don't have enough time, money, talent, knowledge, or guts to start your own business.
- See yourself reaching down and lifting these heavy rocks into the box, one at a time. Include feelings such as disappointment, fear, anger, and resentment and place them inside the box too.
- When you are finished, close the top so that your doubts and fears cannot get out.
- Now imagine a large, strong, shiny pink bubble surrounding the box that contains your doubts and fears.
- See the bubble grow larger until it lifts the box and its contents into the air. Watch the box and the shiny pink bubble float off into the distance until they are out of sight—and out of your mind!

TECHNIQUE #3: USE AFFIRMATIONS TO PROMOTE POSITIVE SELF-TALK

Affirmations are confidence-building statements or self-talk that you say to yourself either aloud or silently. Your mind is constantly chattering with itself, even though you may not be fully aware of the inner conversation's content or focus. All too often this "self-talk" raises doubts, worries, and other counterproductive thoughts that inhibit your creativity, hinder your progress, and block your achievement. Affirmations are a way of replacing old self-talk patterns of disapproval and skepticism with more optimistic suggestions that promote success.

As with visualization, place your affirmations in the present tense. Affirmations can, over time, help transform your negative attitudes and low expectations into the realm of the positive and possible. Make your affirmations short in length and phrase them in a way that says what you want—not what you don't want. Here are a few examples of the right and wrong way to use self-talk, or affirmations, before discussing a proposal with your boss.

Strong Affirmation	Weak Affirmation
"I am calm, *prepared, and confident.*"	"*I hope I don't forget my presentation.*"
"*I am confident that this is a great proposal.*"	"*I'm pretty sure this proposal will work.*"
"*I welcome feedback.*"	"*I hope she won't be critical.*"
"*I'm pleased that my boss likes this proposal.*"	"*If I'm lucky, my boss might like this proposal.*"
"*I'm happy my boss is comfortable sharing her thoughts with me.*"	"*I wish she didn't make me feel so nervous when she talks to me.*"
"*I enjoy sharing ideas with my boss.*"	"*I hope my boss doesn't make too many suggestions.*"

TECHNIQUE #4: SCRIPTING A COMMUNICATION GAME PLAN

Scripting, or writing out what you want to say, helps you stay calm in difficult conversations because it provides a game plan for you to follow when you talk. Saying what you mean with confidence is tough under the best of circumstances, but it is even more difficult if you just "wing it" or only react to someone's attacks or objections. Knowing what you are going to say also allows you to keep focused on the "big picture" and not get sidetracked into counterproductive arguments over irrelevant details. In addition, scripting your communication helps clarify your thoughts and feelings so that when you express them aloud, you do so with confidence.

Let's say, for example, that you feel strongly about the need for you and your spouse to see a therapist to help work out some problems in your marriage. You are nervous about bringing up the subject because the last time you tried, you "beat around the bush" and ended up fighting with your spouse about everything except getting some marriage counseling. This time, however, you prepare a script that follows a simple format: (1) Get to the point; (2) present the reasons for your views; (3) give specific examples; and (4) repeat your conclusions and the additional steps you want to take.

Here is the script you might write using this approach to help you present your ideas more clearly when you speak to your spouse:

Step 1: Get to the point right away and reveal your opinion of the situation. Never wait until the end of your conversation or evening to say what it's all about. For example:

> *"I'll get right to the point, and please hear me out. I'm worried about our marriage and I think we could use some help in working out some of our problems. I'd like for us to see a marriage counselor."*

Step 2: Be brief. Use short words and sentences, give the reasons behind your opinion, and state what you want. For example:

> *"I believe that for a marriage to succeed, both people have to want it to work. Let's face it, both of us have put our careers first and our marriage on the back burner. We never see each other, and when we do, we frequently argue. I want to get our priorities straightened out and get our marriage back on track."*

Step 3: Give specific examples to illustrate your point and include names, dates, and numbers. For example:

> *"Let me give you a few examples of what I'm talking about. Do you know that in the last three months we've had over twenty major arguments! I know, because I wrote about them in my diary! Plus it seems as if we're either too busy or too tired to go out and have fun together anymore. We even canceled our anniversary dinner because we were both too exhausted from work! I'm afraid that if we don't make some changes in our work schedules, our marriage is going to be canceled permanently for lack of interest!"*

Step 4: Repeat your point of view and conclusion, emphasizing the next step. For example:

"I've concluded that if this marriage is going to succeed, we are going to need some professional help—fast! I've called a highly recommended marriage counselor who said she will see us next Tuesday evening from seven to eight p.m. I'm going, for sure, and I would like you to come with me. What do you think? How about giving it a shot?"

While most discussions do not follow written formats like this, scripting a communication game plan keeps you stay focused and composed in difficult conversations. It provides a framework with which you can organize your ideas, articulate your goals, present your case, and say what you mean in a calm, orderly, and confident manner.

TECHNIQUE #5: PRACTICING YOUR PRESENTATION

Practicing what you want to say before you go into a difficult conversation helps keep you calm because it allows you to internalize and adopt your communication game plan. As an effective communicator, *how* you speak is more important than *what* you actually say. Studies show that your body language and tone of voice account for about 90 percent of your total message. As little as 10 percent of your message is based on the words you say.

Use the following practice techniques and you will deliver a message that radiates confidence and conviction!

1. Practice Out Loud

- Hear the sound of your voice.
- Emphasize the words in your message that are most important. For example: ***"I want to be considered for the job.***
- Speak slowly and deliberately.
- Say aloud, ***"I sound calm and confident."***

2. Use a Mirror to Observe How Others See You

- Establish eye contact. This is especially important when you begin speaking, when you are making a main point, and at the end of your message.

- Relax the muscles around your eyes, mouth, neck, and shoulders.
- Keep your arms uncrossed. Gesture with your hands to emphasize a point.
- Keep your head upright, looking proud and confident.
- Say aloud, *"I look in control and confident."*

3. Practice Often

- Rehearse your script at least five times before saying it "for real."
- Practice in front of a friend or into a tape recorder.
- Rehearse your script right up to the time you are ready to speak.
- Say aloud, *"Each time I say what I mean, I feel more composed and confident. I am communicating effectively."*

You won't be able to deal with all difficult conversations by writing a script and rehearsing it. However, those planned confrontations present excellent opportunities to build your skills and confidence so that you can face "unexpected" verbal confrontations more comfortably. You can also build your confidence by speaking assertively in various low-risk situations before taking on high-risk, difficult conversations.

AN EXTRA-TOUGH GOAL: KEEPING CALM IN UNEXPECTED CONFRONTATIONS

How do you react if someone takes you by surprise and confronts you with angry words? Do you grit your teeth, clinch your fists, and fight, or do you panic and make a hasty retreat? Fortunately there is an alternative strategy for coping with unexpected verbal confrontations that allows you to regain your composure, remain calm, and defuse an emotionally challenging situation.

Use this four-point strategy: (1) Don't fight back; (2) exercise self-control; (3) listen, sympathize, and acknowledge feelings; and (4) guide the other person to an acceptable compromise.

Step 1: Don't Fight Back

When you come under verbal attack, your body immediately reacts by pumping adrenaline into your bloodstream in preparation for an impending fight. Your forehead and ears get hot, your eyes narrow, your heart beats more rapidly, and your blood pressure goes sky-high. Meanwhile your mind races to find ammunition to throw back at the person who verbally assaulted you, because you've been taught that "a good offense is the best defense." The result? The fight is on, but few confrontations stop at this point. More frequently the insults and accusations become more volatile until someone says a regrettable statement such as *"I've always thought you were a jerk!"* or *"I knew I should never have hired you!"* Once confrontations reach this level, it is nearly impossible to remain cool and calm. There are no winners—only losers who go home licking their wounds.

You can, however, maintain your composure during unexpected confrontations if you don't fight back. Instead adopt an attitude that verbal attacks do not require an immediate counterattack. The best response to a verbal assault by your boss, lover, parent, or anyone else, is to do *nothing*—except listen. Take a few deep breaths to help you relax and collect your thoughts. Make it your goal to understand the nature of the attack so that you can find a reasonable compromise that both of you can live with. Here are statements that say you are not going to fight back in response to a verbal attack:

> *"I don't want to get into a fight with you about this, but I do want to hear what you have to say."*

> *"I'm not going to argue with you about it, but I do want to understand why you think that way."*

Step 2: Exercise Self-control

How do you keep yourself from fighting with an attacker? By exercising self-control. It will help you regain your composure after the shock of an unexpected verbal assault. Rather than flying off the handle in response to another person's hostility, try to relax and focus your attention on the reasons for the conflict. Then set the ground rules of how you are going to communicate by telling your attacker:

"I'm not going to get upset, because I want to talk about this problem rationally."

"I'm going to stay calm, because I communicate better that way."

"Let's try to leave personalities out of this and stick to the issues."

"I'm not going to lose my temper, because I don't want to say anything that I'll regret later."

"Why don't you take a moment and calm down. Then we'll talk."

Step 3: Listen, Sympathize, and Acknowledge Feelings

An effective method for keeping your cool with an angry person is to concede his right to feel the way he does, even if you disagree. Using an "acknowledgment strategy" allows you to remain calm and objective without having to defend yourself. Then using reflective listening skills show that you sympathize with and understand your attacker's feelings. This action tends to defuse the conflict. A sympathetic response keeps you from fighting with the person and allows you to zero in on the sources of the conflict. Here are some examples of statements that acknowledge another person's feelings:

"After telling you that you got left behind, I can see why you are feeling upset."

"Now that I know you are interested in me, it makes perfect sense that you would be upset by me ignoring you."

"If I saw that kind of sloppy painting done in my house, I'd be angry about it too."

"I'd be furious, too, if I heard someone was talking about me like that."

"From what you've described, I think you have a perfect right to be upset."

When you remain composed under pressure, it also encourages the other person to calm down and talk more rationally. By carefully listening you may discover that the angry person has:

• Magnified an incident out of proportion
• Misunderstood information
• Interpreted your statement or action as a personal attack
• Picked a fight to cover up a larger issue
• Made you aware of a genuine complaint that you need to address

Listening, sympathizing, and acknowledging a person's feelings defuses hostility and gives you more time to get the facts and assess the situation so that you can decide how to respond to the specific issues.

Step 4: Guide the Other Person to an Acceptable Compromise

Once you determine the source of conflict by seeing the situation from the other person's perspective, you can find a compromise that satisfies both of you. Now that you have defused a tense situation, you have the opportunity to discuss possible outcomes and solutions to the problem. Impress upon the other person that to work out a true compromise, each of you needs to look at the issues from the other's perspective. Once you explore the specific issues and focus on the problems—not the personalities—then solutions for compromise will surface. Using this process—the fine art of deal making—both people walk away from what was once a hostile situation feeling satisfied with the results.

You might guide the other person into talking about solutions or a compromise by saying:

"Now that we both understand the issue better, let's see if we can come up with some solutions that will make both of us happy."

"I'm sure we can iron out our differences on this problem."

"I can understand that you feel that everything is getting dumped on you. If we both take a look at all the work that needs to be done, I'm sure we can work out a better way to share the load."

"When you're not happy, I'm not happy. Let's start talking again so that we can figure out a way to get this relationship back on track."

STAYING CALM IN CONFLICT INCREASES YOUR PERSONAL POWER

Your confidence and personal power are grounded in the knowledge that when issues that create conflict arise, you can deal with them in a controlled and reasonable manner. Relaxing your body and mind, visualizing positive results, using affirmative self-talk, scripting your communication game plan, and rehearsing sets the stage for success in challenging conversations. Not fighting back, exercising self-control, listening, sympathizing, acknowledging, and guiding the other person to an acceptable compromise complete the strategies necessary to stay calm and communicate effectively in even the most difficult of verbal confrontations.

CHAPTER 4

Becoming an Assertive Communicator

Are you a wimp when it comes to standing up to a conversational bully? Are you afraid to say no to even the most outlandish requests? Do you cringe at the thought of confronting someone who is making your life miserable? If you allow aggressive sales people, manipulative relatives, or hostile coworkers to take advantage of you, then it's time for you to learn how to tap the power of assertive communication skills.

What does it mean to be assertive? To begin with, this often misused term does *not* mean being aggressive. Speaking assertively means that you can make a positive statement or request and then be ready to respond to a possible objection, refusal, or disapproval from the listener. When you make an assertive statement, it suggests that you have high self-esteem, strong beliefs, and will assume personal responsibility for your words and actions. It is your assertiveness and persistence—*not* how aggressively you speak or act—that reflect your confidence.

WHAT CAN ASSERTIVE COMMUNICATION DO FOR YOU?

Mastering the art of assertive communication can help you in many ways. You have your own goals, needs, and priorities, which may lead to conflict with others around you. Assertive communication allows people with different viewpoints and goals to minimize friction by reaching mutually acceptable compromises.

48

By using both assertiveness and tact in stressful conversations you can get your points across to others without resorting to shouting or insensitive comments. When you speak assertively, others are more likely to listen and respect your feelings, opinions, judgments, and viewpoints. Plus, they will be more open to changing their behavior or how they treat you.

As you may have guessed, assertiveness skills and self-esteem are closely linked. There is no doubt that your self-esteem suffers whenever your boss, coworkers, relatives, friends, or business associates coerce you into doing something you'd rather not do. On the other hand, your self-esteem and confidence increase when you assertively stand up for yourself—at home, at work, or in the business world.

How Assertive Are You?

Take this short quiz and find out. Use the scale below. Write 0, 1, 2, 3, or 4 in the space after each question, then total your score. See the evaluation at the end of the quiz to rate your assertiveness skills.

0 = Never 1 = Rarely 2 = Sometimes 3 = Frequently 4 = Always

1. Do you get tongue-tied or offended if someone questions your judgment, decisions, opinions, or feelings? _____

2. Do you let others take advantage of your good nature or make you feel guilty for not coming to their rescue? _____

3. Do you get stuck with unpleasant jobs at work because you're afraid to say no to your supervisor or coworkers? _____

4. Do you avoid making personal decisions or pursuing your dreams because you might be criticized by your friends or family? _____

5. Do salespeople talk you into purchasing products or services that you never planned on buying and don't really need? _____

6. Is it difficult for you to criticize other people's actions, even when they affect you adversely? _____

7. Do you avoid telling friends and family why you are angry? _____

8. Do you have difficulty expressing your opinions and feelings in groups or on a one-to-one basis? _____

9. Do you avoid complaining to managers about poor customer service in restaurants or other businesses?

10. Do you remain nearly silent in conversations so that you won't say the wrong thing or offend the other person? _____

Score:

0–10 YOUR ASSERTIVENESS SKILLS ARE EXCELLENT: Congratulations! You are a confident individual who knows how to stick up for yourself in any demanding conversation. Keep up the good work!

11–16 YOUR ASSERTIVENESS SKILLS ARE GOOD: All right! You are your own person most of the time, but you still allow yourself to be manipulated under more stressful circumstances.

17–25 YOUR ASSERTIVENESS SKILLS ARE FAIR: Not too bad! You speak your mind about half the time, but frequently think of what you could have said after the conversation is over.

26–34 YOUR ASSERTIVENESS SKILLS NEED MORE PRACTICE: You don't stand up for yourself enough. People know that if they push you long enough and hard enough, you'll cave in and do what they want. You need to use the power of persistence.

35–40 YOU NEED TO LEARN BASIC ASSERTIVENESS SKILLS: People see you as a pushover and take full advantage of you—only because you let them. You can change that perception if you make it your goal to become an assertive communicator.

DEVELOP ASSERTIVENESS SKILLS AT ANY STAGE OF YOUR LIFE

Assertiveness skills are easy to learn and make a big difference in how you feel about yourself and how others treat you. After using the following six-step assertiveness strategy, take this quiz again and see how much better you do. It does take practice to become an assertive communicator, but the boost it gives your self-esteem makes it well worth the effort!

A Six-Step Assertiveness Strategy

The following six-step assertiveness strategy provides an example that shows how to handle a difficult conversation. Although all six steps are illustrated in this example, it is not always necessary to use all of them, and you can change the order to suit your own particular situation. Keep in mind, however, that it is vital to get to the "bottom line" of what you want to say *before* the other person pleads innocence, counterattacks, or changes the subject.

In addition, avoid starting the conversation if you sense that your emotions are bubbling just below the surface or you feel so angry, you are just waiting to explode. Instead of facing off in a verbal duel, take a short walk and spend several minutes breathing deeply to regain control of your feelings before approaching the other person. Even though you may still be angry or annoyed, speaking calmly improves your ability to communicate, encourages receptivity in others, and allows both of you to remain dignified and tactful.

Situation: You and a coworker share a ride to your place of employment. Your coworker is frequently not ready when you drive up to his house in the morning, and he is frequently late in picking you up for work. Your coworker's tardiness has caused you to be late several times, and today you got reprimanded by your boss. Yes, it does take courage to confront someone, so begin by reinforcing your right to address and resolve issues that affect you.

STEP 1: REPEAT YOUR ASSERTIVENESS RIGHTS TO YOURSELF

Before you confront your coworker, say the following to yourself:

"I have a right to think, feel, and act the way I do."

"I have a right to change my mind."

"I have a right to be treated with respect."

"I have a right to say no."

"I have a right to act on my own behalf."

STEP 2: REQUEST A PRIVATE MOMENT

In a calm tone tell your coworker:

"I need to talk to you about a problem. Do you have a few minutes?"

STEP 3: BRIEFLY DESCRIBE THE PROBLEM BEHAVIOR

Continue talking in a firm, but friendly tone:

"I like sharing rides to work with you, but over the last few weeks, I've been late to work at least half a dozen times because either you haven't been ready to leave on time when I pick you up or you have arrived late when it's your turn to drive and pick me up."

STEP 4: SAY HOW THE PROBLEM BEHAVIOR ADVERSELY AFFECTS YOU

Stick to the point. Let the tone, not the volume, of your voice convey your concern. Say:

"Arriving twenty to thirty minutes late causes me major problems because it puts me behind schedule for the whole day. Plus, this morning my boss gave me an 'official warning,' as she put it, because I was late for the sixth time this month!"

STEP 5: STATE WHAT THE PARTICULAR BEHAVIOR IS YOU WANT TO CHANGE

Keep your voice firm and your body language open. Get to the bottom line and emphasize key words such as "leaving between seven-thirty and seven forty-five," "carpool with me," "not ready," and "getting to work on your own." Say:

> *"Maybe you're not worried about staying on good terms with your supervisor, but I am with mine. So, from now on, I'm LEAVING at our regular time—BETWEEN SEVEN-THIRTY AND SEVEN FORTY-FIVE A.M. If you still want to CARPOOL WITH ME, that's great, but if you're NOT READY to go by then, you can plan on GETTING TO WORK ON YOUR OWN."*

STEP 6: REPEAT YOUR POSITION AND ASK FOR A RESPONSE

Smile and gesture with your hands open, palms facing upward. Say:

> *"You know, I enjoy your company, but I can't afford to arrive late to work anymore. So what do you want to do— keep riding to work together or commute on our own?"*

Handling Resistance With the "Broken Record" Technique

Hopefully your coworker will agree to get his act together and be on time from now on. You must be prepared, however, for a more common response, such as feeble excuses, arguments, or accusations that attempt to minimize the situation. They might sound like this:

> *"Hey, I haven't been late all that many times!"*

> *"I remember you were late once too!"*

> *"We were stuck in traffic last week. You can't blame that one on me!"*

"Your supervisor really has you under her thumb, doesn't she?"

"She's just trying to make you jump and let everyone know that she's in charge."

"It's just a lot of hot air. Don't worry about it."

"Tell her it's my fault and she'll let you off the hook."

"Don't be so paranoid! This job isn't that great anyhow."

Don't argue—simply repeat your bottom line like a "broken record." While you might be tempted to defend yourself against accusations such as *"Why do you want to be on time? Are you bucking for a promotion?"* your best bet is to use the highly effective "broken record" assertiveness strategy. This assertiveness skill consists of repeating more or less the same answer over and over again without further elaboration—like a broken record—until the other person accepts your position and deals with the issue. Keep your voice and body language friendly, but get to the point as quickly as you can. It might sound something like this:

"I can see how you might think that, but let me repeat what I said. From now on, I'm leaving at our regular time— between seven-thirty and seven forty-five a.m. If you still want to ride to work together, you're going to be ready to go by then or plan on getting to work on your own. So what do you want to do, keep riding to work together or commute on our own?"

When Saying No Once, Twice, or Even Three Times Doesn't Work

You can use the "broken record" technique for rude people who do not know how to take no for an answer. Whether you are refusing food, alcohol, drugs, a date, or anything else, the "broken record" technique of saying no is very effective. Here is another example:

Him: *"Hi there. Hey, you need a drink!"*

Her: *"No, thank you. I don't care for anything to drink right now."*

Him: *"How about a wine cooler? They're really good!"*

Her: *"Thanks for asking, but I don't care for anything to drink right now."*

Him: *"Oh, come on. Here, take this beer."*

Her: *"No, thank you, I'd rather not. I don't care for anything to drink right now."*

Him: *"Why not, are you afraid you might like it?"*

Her: *"I just don't care for anything to drink right now. Do you have a problem with that?"*

Him: *"One lousy drink isn't going to hurt you. Come on, loosen up a little and have some fun!"*

Her: *"No, thanks. I really don't care for a drink right now."*

Him (frustrated:) *"Well, then, I'm leaving!"*

TALK ASSERTIVELY, NOT AGGRESSIVELY

Aggressive statements often contain criticisms and accusations, while assertive statements reveal a speaker's feelings and wishes. The following "Don't Say" examples are aggressive and can provoke arguments. If they are replaced by the more open-minded and assertive "Do Say" examples, there is a better chance that the listener will be more open and thus respond positively.

You Don't Say . . . Or Do You?

Don't Say . . .	Do Say . . .
"You should know how I feel."	*"I'm upset because. . . ."*
"You shouldn't feel bad."	*"How do you feel about the situation now?"*
"Why do you always blame me when something goes wrong?"	*"I'd like to tell you my side of the story."*
"What makes you so smart?"	*"You've made a good point."*
"I told you so."	*"It could happen to anyone."*
"How could you be so stupid as to think that?"	*"I don't see the situation the way you do, but I respect your opinion."*

SOME MORE ASSERTIVENESS TIPS

Beware of always having to get your way. Flexibility and compromise are as important as assertiveness in any conversation. Say,

"I'm willing to talk about it."

When someone attempts to control your behavior through guilt-inducing statements or threats, say,

"I do not respond to or appreciate this kind of manipulation."

When someone asks you something and expects a quick response, give yourself a moment or two to gather your thoughts. Say,

"Let me think about what you've said for a moment before I give you my answer."

When you find yourself under pressure from someone asking you to do something you don't want to do, stand up straight, look him or her in the eye, and with a firm voice repeat as often as necessary:

> *"I understand what you are asking me to do, but the answer is no."*

Begin your assertiveness training right now by repeating this statement to yourself several times a day:

> *"I have the right to think and feel the way I do, and if other people can't accept that, it's their problem, not mine!"*

ASSERTIVENESS GETS RESULTS

You may be surprised to find out how effective assertiveness statements are—as long as you are fair and say them clearly and calmly. Most people feel embarrassed to hear that they were tactless or caused you a problem. If the other person cares about you at all, he or she will quickly apologize and bend over backward to make amends. When this happens, show that you know how to accept an apology and say,

> *"Thanks! I appreciate your listening to me. As far as I'm concerned, the case is closed."*

CHAPTER 5

Coping with Prickly Personalities

Certain irksome people will test the mettle of your assertiveness skills and the limits of your patience again and again! These difficult personalities batter your feelings and trample on your self-esteem—if you let them get away with it. While everyone can be annoying at times, the following prickly personalities are tough to deal with and require extra perseverance and additional coping strategies. They are: the Steamroller, the Know-It-All, the Bushwhacker, and the Wet Blanket.

THE STEAMROLLER

Steamrollers are pushy people who aim to prove they are right and get their way through intense pressure, threats, and intimidation. These hostile and often abusive people scream accusations at the top of their lungs and pound their fists on the table with the hope that you'll cave in and do things their way. Their goal is to flatten any opposition, and by the time you know what has hit you, a Steamroller can quickly level you and your self-esteem!

A Steamroller sounds something like this:

"How could you be so stupid!"

"You're going to pay for this!"

"If you don't do as I say, you're going to regret it."

"You'd better do what I want, or there's going to be hell to pay!"

"This is what you're going to do. I don't want to hear another word!"

The next time someone with a steamroller personality tries to flatten you, use this three-step strategy: (1) Disagree, but don't argue; (2) ask "Why do you feel that way?" questions; (3) take your turn to talk.

Step 1: Disagree, But Don't Argue

Steamrollers want to dominate others and they know they can get away with their aggressive tactics because many people would rather give in to their pressure than get into a knock-down-drag-out fight. Steamrollers count on a desire on the part of others to avoid confrontation, but they get thrown off their guard when someone unexpectedly disagrees. When you stick up for yourself, it tells the person with a Steamroller personality that you are not going to let him or her push you around.

How do you stick up for yourself when you are in the path of a Steamroller? Unfold your arms, make steady eye contact, say the Steamroller's name, and tell him or her that you disagree—but don't get into a fight. Here are some ways to disagree:

"Father-in-law, I disagree with you."

"Mom, I see the situation differently."

"Mr. Neighbor, I don't see it that way. In my opinion . . ."

"Boss, with all due respect, it's my view that . . ."

"Mrs. Customer, it's my understanding that . . ."

AVOID "FIGHTIN' " WORDS

Disagree, but don't fight with a Steamroller for these two excellent reasons: They love to fight and they usually win. If you avoid statements that provoke arguments, you can stick up for yourself and prevent the Steamroller from getting worked up. Let the Steamroller know that you disagree, but do so in a way that avoids an argument. *Avoid* provocative statements such as:

"You're dead wrong."

"You're full of beans."

"What makes you think you're so smart?"

"You'd better watch what you say to me!"

"I don't have to listen to this garbage!"

"Who do you think you are talking to?"

Step 2: Ask "Why Do You Feel That Way?" Questions

After saying, *"I disagree,"* ask the Steamroller to expand on his or her viewpoint. This shows you are willing to listen and would rather understand an opposing view or opinion than argue about who is right. You can say:

"I disagree with you, but please tell me why you think that way."

"I don't share your opinion, but I'd like to know why you feel the way you do."

"I have a different opinion, but can you give me an insight into the reasons why you see the issue as you do?"

Step 3: Take Your Turn to Talk

After the Steamroller has expressed his or her views, it is crucial that you take your turn to speak, because if you don't, the Steamroller will start putting the pressure on you again. In addition, when you talk, it takes the control away from the Steamroller and clearly demonstrates that you are not intimidated by aggressive tactics.

AGREE WITH A POINT, THEN PRESENT YOUR VIEW

If you begin your rebuttal by acknowledging a point—even a minor point—that the Steamroller made earlier, he or she will be confused because you are agreeing and disagreeing at the same time. You can say something like:

"While I agree with you that . . . , I've come to a different conclusion."

"What you said about . . . makes perfect sense, but I see it having a slightly different impact than you suggest."

"I couldn't agree with you more about . . . , but I don't see that as something negative. In fact, rather the opposite, because. . . ."

DON'T LET THE STEAMROLLER INTERRUPT YOU

Steamrollers almost always interrupt the people they are trying to manipulate, but don't let them get away with that intimidating tactic. Stop the interrupting Steamroller by first saying his or her name and saying:

"Mrs. Smith, you interrupted me. I am explaining the situation to you, so please listen."

Don't say, **"Quit interrupting me"** or **"Stop interrupting me"** or **"You never let me finish talking!"** because those provoking words challenge the Steamroller to fight on. Just repeat, **"Mr. . . . , you interrupted me. I was saying. . . ."** each time the Steamroller interrupts, until he or she stops trying to take the conversational ball away from you.

This assertive strategy makes the Steamroller aware that you are not going to cave in from his or her pressure, but that you are not interested in an argument either. In most cases, once you stand up to Steamrollers they will respect you more and attempt to intimidate you less. Plus, your self-esteem will grow and you'll be more confident when dealing with other prickly personalities.

THE KNOW-IT-ALL

Know-It-Alls feel compelled to impress and dominate you with what they believe to be their vast experience and superior knowledge. Know-It-Alls like to see themselves as experts and believe that they always have the right answer to any problem! While they may be well-meaning, Know-It-Alls try to overwhelm you with facts to prove they are right, minimize your level of understanding, and pressure you into accepting their expert advice.

Know-It-Alls sound something like this:

"Listen to me, kid, because when it comes to . . . , I know what I'm talking about."

"It's pretty obvious that you don't have a clue as to what this issue is all about. You'd better let me make this decision for you."

"I'll tell you exactly what you should do."

"Look, let me explain it so that even a simpleton like you can understand!"

You can question the wisdom of the Know-It-All's advice without getting into an argument or making him or her feel snubbed and insulted. This three-step strategy can help you tactfully cope with a pushy Know-It-All: (1) Restate the main points; (2) ask detailed follow-up questions; (3) ask for a solution to a worst-case scenario.

Step 1: Restate the Main Points

Restating the Know-It-All's main points shows you are listening and that you understand what he or she has told you. If you fail to use this reflective-listening skill, you are sure to get a blast of,

"Well, I can see I'm going to have to explain the whole thing to you again!" For example, if the Know-It-All is pressuring you to invest in a high-risk stock instead of a tax-free bond, you can say:

> *"Let me see if I understand you correctly. I stand to make twenty percent on my money if I invest in Hi-Jinx stocks instead of only six percent on tax-free bonds. That's a difference of fourteen percent, right?"*

Step 2: Ask Detailed Follow-up Questions

Asking follow-up questions shows that you are considering what the Know-It-All has suggested, but also indicates that you are still a little fuzzy on some of the finer points. Know-It-Alls love the sound of their own voice, so be prepared for more facts and figures. For instance you can ask:

> *"There is still something I don't quite understand, and I'm sure you can explain to me. If I invest in this stock and it goes up like you said it would, how much is my profit after I pay taxes and how do I figure that out?"*

Step 3: Ask a "What if . . . ?" Worst-Case Scenario Question

Know-It-Alls are very impressed with their own logic, so give them a worst-case scenario based on the situation under discussion and then let them problem-solve a possible solution. Here is an example of what to say:

> *"I know you said it's just a matter of time before the value of the Hi-Jinx stock skyrockets, but let me ask you this hypothetical question. What if Hi-Jinx stock increases only at about the same rate as inflation? What other ways could I invest my money so that I'm not putting all my eggs in one basket?"*

Once you get Know-It-Alls to consider worst-case scenarios and come up with other possibilities, they will often back off on pressing you to follow their expert advice—at least for the moment!

THE BUSHWHACKER

Bushwhackers can be deadly because they ambush you with innuendos, sarcastic remarks, and humor—at your expense! Unlike Steamrollers or Know-It-Alls, who use head-to-head confrontations to get their way, Bushwhackers are devious and use indirect attacks to chip away at your credibility. They much prefer playing to an audience and camouflaging their assaults so that they can boost their status while putting you on the spot.

A Bushwhacker's sarcasm sounds something like this:

"You brought that pink cake for the party? Who made it for you, your kid? (ha-ha-ha!)"

"You landed the Jones account? Then it's true what they say about you and old man Jones! (ha-ha-ha!)"

"Oh, a new dress! Did your husband finally break down, or do you have a secret 'friend' who buys you clothes on sale at K-Mart? (ha-ha-ha!)"

If you say nothing to Bushwhackers when they attack you, be prepared for their mocking comments to continue. You can, however, use this four-step strategy to stop Bushwhackers in their tracks: (1) Confront the Bushwhacker; (2) ask for negative feedback; (3) ask others for input; (4) continue your presentation.

Step 1: Confront the Bushwhacker

Most Bushwhackers hate direct confrontation, so force them out into the open from behind their sarcastic remarks or innuendos. It is easier to challenge the Bushwhacker in private, but if your credibility is on the line in a sales meeting, for example, confront the Bushwhacker right then and there. Whether you confront the Bushwhacker in private or public, your coworkers and friends will observe how you handle (or don't handle) these quietly aggressive people and will either respect or condemn you based on your actions.

Here is an example of a Bushwhacker in a business situation: Let's say you are making a sales presentation before a group of coworkers and a Bushwhacker starts making nasty comments and little jokes from the back of the room. Stop your presentation, look the Bushwhacker in the eye, smile, and say,

> *"Excuse me, Phil, but I heard you say something but didn't quite catch the whole thing. What was it you said?"*

> *"Phil, if you have a question or comment to contribute, why don't you say it so that everyone can hear? Go ahead, you've got the floor."*

Sometimes by simply drawing attention to the Bushwhacker, he or she will back off, but you must be prepared for more sarcastic comments, snide remarks, and more laughs—at your expense. It is good to show your sense of humor, but now it's your turn to put the pressure on the Bushwhacker.

Step 2: Ask for Negative Feedback

Asking a *"What is it about . . . that you don't like?"* question puts the conversational ball square in the court of the Bushwhacker and forces him or her to make specific comments openly, which you can then address. Here are some words you can use to show your sense of humor while forcing the Bushwhacker to own up to his or her comments:

> *"Phil, your comment about my plan was very funny, but I'm picking up a distinct feeling that you're not crazy about my idea. If I'm right about that, why don't you tell me and the rest of us what it is that you don't like?"*

> *"Phil, remind me to let you do your comedy routine at the next awards dinner, but for right now I'm still getting the feeling from your remarks that you don't think much of*

this idea. If that's how you feel, I want to hear what's bothering you so that we can discuss it."

(Pause and let the silence hang a bit longer than necessary. Everyone in the room will be waiting for the Bushwhacker to respond, but chances are he or she will back down.)

Step 3: Ask Others for Input

Once the Bushwhacker backs down, ask the other people in the room for their input. Encouraging open discussion at this point will often bring out your allies, and if other critical comments come up, then you can use the group to problem-solve and find a solution. Here's what to say:

"How do the rest of you feel about this idea? Do you like it? Do you think it will work? Do you hate it? Any ideas to improve it? Let's open the subject to discussion."

Step 4: Continue Your Presentation

Now that you have cut off the Bushwhacker's power over the meeting, move your presentation forward with gusto. Don't make a big deal about the confrontation with the Bushwhacker, and at the conclusion of the meeting thank everyone present who made a contribution. Here's what you can say:

"Well, now that we've agreed that this proposal is worth pursuing, I'll be getting back to you soon for more ideas. I want to thank you all (establish eye contact with the Bushwhacker) for your input because everyone's opinion is important.

Confronting a Bushwhacker in Private

There are times when it is more appropriate to confront a Bushwhacker in private. For instance, maybe a friend or family member puts you on the spot in a restaurant, and you don't want to make a scene. Later in private you can say:

"Joan, during lunch yesterday with Aunt Lucy and Cousin Sarah you made that little joke about my new dress and a 'friend.' What I want to know is, were you trying to stir up some family trouble? Do you want to tell me what was in your mind?"

Whether you confront the Bushwhacker in public or in private, be prepared for him or her to react defensively, deny all wrongdoing, and say with a nervous laugh:

"Of course I was joking! Oh, come on, don't be so sensitive! What's the matter, can't you take a little teasing?"

Then give the Bushwhacker your best stare, a clever smile, and say:

"Sure I can, but I picked up a definite feeling that you were trying to put me on the spot with the rest of the family (or staff, friends, or whomever). *Why would you say something like that to me?"*

In most cases, when you confront Bushwhackers, they will retreat for a while until the next situation comes up when they can return to their old tricks! When the Bushwhacker strikes again, be ready to strike back!

THE WET BLANKET

Wet Blankets are gloomy people who constantly deflate other people's dreams or goals. They habitually bring up innumerable reasons not to do things or take risks and quickly proclaim their philosophy: *"It's not going to work anyway, so why bother?"* Wet Blankets not only sap their own motivation but they also turn off and undermine the enthusiasm of everyone else around them. Since a Wet Blanket's negativity is contagious, these naysayers can make people miss opportunities, can squelch their dreams, and can stunt their potential.

Wet Blankets have a negative attitude that spreads like a dark cloud over any idea. You'll hear them saying demoralizing comments such as:

"You want to do what?"

"Why bother? No one will notice anyhow."

"Who cares about that, anyway?"

"You couldn't do that in a million years. You're nothing but a dreamer."

"What makes you think you can succeed when a lot of other people ten times more talented and intelligent than you have failed?"

Use this four-step strategy to counter the Wet Blanket's cynical attitude: (1) Don't argue, rather listen and rephrase; (2) acknowledge the Wet Blanket's viewpoint; (3) say you are going to take the risk anyway; and (4) ask the Wet Blanket to help you.

Step 1: Don't Argue, Rather Listen and Rephrase

Wet Blankets have an unlimited supply of reasons for not doing things. Arguing only stimulates more negativity. Instead of arguing with a Wet Blanket, rephrase what he or she has said and zero in on the key points. Here are some examples of what you can say to show you are listening:

"If I understand you correctly, you think that New York has more out-of-work actors and singers than any city in the United States. Is that what you're saying?"

"Let me see if I understand you. It's your opinion that there isn't a snowball's chance in hell of this project getting our boss's approval. Is that right?"

"From what you've said, you think that I ought to give up my lifelong dream of starting my own business. Did I understand you correctly?"

Step 2: Acknowledge the Wet Blanket's Viewpoint

Acknowledging a Wet Blanket's opinions and views satisfies his or her desire to be heard. Even though they are usually pessimists, Wet Blankets' views can be quite perceptive and helpful. To acknowledge a Wet Blanket's opinion, you can say something like,

> *"You might be right . . . that Broadway doesn't need another actor, but. . . ."*

> *"You are probably right that it will never work, but. . . ."*

> *"It's most likely true that the odds of succeeding in a new business are against me, but. . . ."*

Step 3: Say You Are Going to Take the Risk Anyway

Once you've acknowledged the Wet Blanket's likelihood of being right, simply say that you are going ahead with your plans, even though you run the risk of failing. Here are some risk-taking statements that can help overcome a Wet Blanket's fear of failure from poisoning your passion to achieve:

> *"I'm going to go ahead and give it a try anyway and see what happens."*

> *"I'm dying to know if this idea will work."*

> *"I'm going to take the risk and see if I can do it."*

To further reinforce your risk-taking attitude, say to yourself and to the Wet Blanket:

> *"I'll never know if it will work or not unless I give it a shot. So why not do it? You never know, stranger things have happened, that's for sure!"*

> *"I'll never forgive myself if I don't try."*

"What's the worst thing that can happen? If I fail, at least I have the satisfaction of knowing that I gave it my best shot!"

Step 4: Ask the Wet Blanket to Help You

Rejecting a Wet Blanket's pessimistic views might elicit his or her desire for your failure, just to prove you wrong. Surprisingly, however, if you ask for help in your quest, the Wet Blanket may forgive you for not following his or her advice and may become a powerful ally in achieving your goals. You can say something like:

"I know you think I'm crazy to give up my job, sell my house, and move to New York, and I appreciate your input, I'm going to do it anyway! Do you want to help me when I have my moving sale?"

"I'm sure that all the things you said about my poor chances of succeeding are true, but I'd still love to have you as a partner on this project. What do you say?"

"I appreciate you trying to save me from the grief of failure, but I've made up my mind to give this dream of starting my own business a try. I know you're not behind the idea a hundred percent, but I sure would welcome any help that you would be willing to offer."

DOS AND DON'TS WHEN DEALING WITH PRICKLY PEOPLE

Do remain persistent even though you may feel like giving in.

Don't respond immediately. Take a deep breath and count to ten.

Do listen for areas of agreement.

Don't fight or get caught up in arguing over details.

Do think about what you want to say and then say it.

Don't be overwhelmed by an aggressive person's behavior.

Do exercise your right to reject a pushy person's advice.

Don't let negative people squelch your enthusiasm or rob you of your dreams.

Do stick up for yourself and verbally aggressive people will respect you and be less inclined to pressure you in the future.

Don't give up on yourself if you get overwhelmed by an aggressive person. Practice your assertive skills and be ready for that person the next time.

PART II

TACTFUL TALK IN THE WORKPLACE AND BUSINESS WORLD

CHAPTER 6

Tactful Ways to Tell Your Boss...

If you are like most working people, you spend at least eight hours a day, or about half of your waking hours, at work—not to mention the extra time you spend thinking about work-related issues. There are bosses who are overly critical, authoritarian, stressed out, disorganized, impatient, pushy, or simply inept. How skillfully you communicate with them affects your productivity, job satisfaction, performance reviews, and rate of advancement.

Talking to your supervisor requires the tact of a diplomat and the timing of a snake wrangler. To get the results you want, approach your supervisor at a convenient time and then briefly and confidently present your case. Above all, avoid angry confrontations, because while you may get some immediate satisfaction from blowing off some steam, you can almost certainly expect a reprisal that may hurt your professional image and your career.

#1 "I DEMAND A RAISE!"

Before you storm into your boss's office demanding more money, remember that your financial problems are not your supervisor's concern. Plus, simply working hard at your job does not necessarily entitle you to a raise. You must persuade your boss—and perhaps your boss's boss—that you are worth more money by presenting specific ways you have saved the company money, cut costs, increased sales and productivity, solved costly problems, and how you can contribute even more.

Promotions are usually accompanied by raises, so if you want more responsibility and more money, then suggest more duties that may lead you to the next position along your career track. Then, when a position becomes available, you have already demonstrated to your boss that you can perform the new tasks and that you are a self-motivated employee. These are the people who usually get the promotions—and consequently the raises.

However, you don't always need a promotion to get a raise. Since your job definition dictates how much you are compensated, rewrite it to reflect more accurately your duties and responsibilities. To find out what your job is really worth, call a few employment agencies, check the classified job advertisements for similar positions, and call your professional association to find the average salary for people who perform tasks comparable to yours. You might even talk to others in your field to find out what is reasonable pay for the job you do, but keep in mind, many people are reluctant to discuss exactly how much money they make.

Now that you are armed with specific examples of your worth, and you have rehearsed what you want to say, you are ready to make your pitch for a raise. To win your case, you must ask your supervisor for about ten minutes of uninterrupted time to discuss an important matter. It is nerve-racking to ask for a raise, so use the relaxation techniques presented in Chapter 3 during the time leading up to your meeting. Remember to inhale deeply and exhale slowly with a hissing sound before you rehearse your script. Visualize yourself talking with ease and confidence right up to the time of your meeting. Roll your head and shoulders to loosen up your neck muscles. Shake your hands and arms to get rid of the jitters. Finally, take one last trip to the rest room to check your appearance and to take a few moments to focus your thoughts once again.

The time has come to go into your boss's office and say,

"I'd like to discuss ways I can move up in our department. I've recently accomplished . . . for the company, but I know I'm capable of much more. I understand a position is opening up soon in our department, and I would like to assume some of its responsibilities now to show you I can do the job. What do you think?"

Or, to ask for a raise directly, you can say,

"I'd like to talk with you about getting a raise. I perform these tasks on a regular basis, all of which exceed my present job description, so I'd like to reclassify my job so that I have more room for advancement."

If your boss says,

"Okay, how much do you want?"

Be ready to respond with a specific dollar figure. You can answer,

"I feel a raise of . . . dollars per hour (month, year) *would be fair, since that is within the pay range in this industry for people doing this kind of work."*

RESPONDING TO YOUR BOSS'S OBJECTIONS

Your boss may reject your request, so anticipate his or her objections and be prepared to respond with suggestions or alternatives. You'll need to adapt the following examples to your own situation, but the idea here is to let your boss know that you are determined to move ahead in your career—and hopefully with your present employer!

Your boss says:

"You want a raise with our budget cuts! There's no way we can afford to give you any more money!"

You can respond:

"I know money is tight. Maybe there are some other ways I can be compensated. How about increasing my commission five percent or giving me an opportunity to handle a larger account?"

Your boss says:

"I'm afraid there aren't any new positions available in this department. In fact we're cutting our staff. You'll have to stay where you are."

You can respond:

> "If that's the case, then perhaps I can move to another department where there is more opportunity for advancement. How would you feel about it if I explored that possibility?"

Your boss says:

> "Well, I wouldn't be happy to see you go because you're one of the best people I have working in my department."

You can respond:

> "I appreciate you saying that about my work, which is exactly why I think I deserve a raise. Can we work something out?"

Your boss says:

> "The problem is if I give you a raise, everyone else in the department will expect one. What am I supposed to say to them?"

You can respond:

> "We're not in a union, and I'm not negotiating a raise for anyone but me. Plus, this isn't something I'm going to go around bragging about. I just want to advance my career opportunities within our company. Is there anything wrong with that?"

Your boss says:

> "There's nothing wrong with wanting to get ahead at work, and you deserve a raise, but I'm sure my boss will say no."

You can respond:

> "I'm glad we agree that I deserve a raise, so why not present my case to your boss? At least she will know how much you value my work. If she does say no, then maybe the two of

*you can think of another way to reward a hardworking
employee like me."*

Your boss says:

*"I'm sorry, I just don't want to give you any false hopes. I
know it is simply impossible to give you a raise, at least not
until our business improves."*

You can respond:

*"I understand. I appreciate your taking the time to discuss
this issue with me. Can we discuss it again in three months
or so?"*

HANDLING A REJECTION

If your request for a raise is denied, it may be tempting to blow
up, threaten to quit, lower your productivity, or sulk at your
desk. However, it is more productive to write a private list of
your options or other employment opportunities and keep the
following points in mind:

- Your boss now knows your career goals and realizes that if
  you are not rewarded, you may seek employment elsewhere.
- Losing good employees makes managers look bad, so take a
  wait-and-see attitude with the hope that your manager may
  find a way of granting your request.
- Don't give up. Keep rewriting your job description, accomplishing project goals, and letting your supervisor know that
  you are persistent in your quest for advancement.

#2 "YOU ARE SO UNFAIR!"

This vague complaint is steeped in frustration. Upon hearing it,
a supervisor may retort, ***"Nobody said life was fair—and everyone knows that work is unfair!"*** Rather than whine like a spoiled
kid, clearly identify your problem and present a possible solution. Be assertive and ask for a few minutes of time alone with
your boss to discuss your sentiments. You can begin by saying:

"Can we get together to talk for a few minutes?"

In private briefly describe the problem and how you think it might be solved. Here are some examples:

"I'm disappointed about not getting my proposal accepted. Will you give me some feedback so that I can improve my chances of getting the next one approved?"

"I'm upset that you were dissatisfied with my report. Will you show me my mistakes so that I can avoid them the next time?"

"I'm more efficient when I'm given specific guidelines and examples to follow along with constructive criticism about my work."

#3 "THESE DEADLINES ARE ABSURD!"

It's Thursday noon and your boss dumps a mountain of files on your desk and says, ***"These are all** top priority **and the client needs to have them first thing tomorrow morning."*** You can curse, skip lunch, work until midnight, and still not finish the task. You can grumble at your boss for asking the impossible, but when the work isn't finished on time, your boss will probably let you have it with both barrels.

Here is a reasonable way to tell your supervisor that the deadlines are either unrealistic or will require reassigning people and setting new priorities. After your boss dumps the assignment on your desk, say:

"I'll be over in a few minutes to give you an idea of when I can get this back to you."

Take a few minutes to estimate the number of hours it will take for you to complete one or two components as well as the entire task. Be sure to figure in extra time for unforeseen difficulties. Then report to your boss with your findings. You can say:

"Mr. Jones, we need to talk about the deadline for this assignment. It takes two hours to process each file, and there are six files. I don't see how I can get this done without . . ."

If your boss interrupts you and says:

"I don't have time for your excuses! I promised the client I'd have those six files on his desk by eight-thirty a.m. If we don't deliver them, I'll look like an idiot, and some heads will roll around here! Just look at all the time you've already wasted! Get back to work!"

You respond with a firm, controlled voice:

"Excuse me Mr. Jones, but you interrupted me. I was about to say that I will need to pull three people from your other project to help me right now if you are going to keep your promise. If that's okay with you, I think we'll be able to make the deadline. We'll send the files out in the last overnight mail."

Your boss pauses, noting that you stood up for yourself and then says:

"Ah . . . well . . . okay. Good idea. Otherwise I'll have to call the client back and make up some lame excuse, and I don't want to do that—again!"

You can also say:

"Mr. Jones, I understand it's hard to say no to a client. I'd like to take a few minutes tomorrow and discuss with you a better plan for completing similar assignments. I have a few ideas that might help prevent these kinds of deadline emergencies from popping up."

Then suggest:

"It would help me a great deal if you could clarify my priorities. Please choose the ONE file that must be completed first. Then list the others in order of importance.

That way we will complete the most important files first and not get caught in a last-minute crunch in the last few hours of the day."

To help your boss set priorities and more realistic deadlines, you can say:

"Mr. Jones, if we have a short meeting every Monday morning to set the week's priorities, then we'll have a better chance of meeting our deadlines in the future."

#4 "I'M NOT WORKING LATE AGAIN!"

What do you do when your boss frequently asks you to work unreasonably long hours? Do you always change your plans or give up time with your family just to finish a task that your boss claims is an emergency, only to be asked the same thing again the next day?

Perhaps your disorganized boss says:

"I'm really behind on my accounts. I want you to work some overtime tonight."

You can respond:

"I wish I could help you out, but I'm afraid that's impossible. I've made plans for tonight that I can't change."

If your boss puts on the pressure and says:

"You're really leaving me in the lurch. Are you sure you can't stay? I'd really appreciate some help."

To avoid being manipulated, you can respond:

"As I said, I've made plans that I can't change, but let me ask around the office to see if anyone wants to put in some overtime. I will do my best to find someone for you."

If your boss makes it a habit of asking you to work late, then negotiate for some extra time off when the workload lightens up. You can say something like:

*"I understand that working overtime is sometimes neces-
sary, but my family and I suffer when I come home late
night after night."*

Your boss responds:

"I'm sorry, but your family problems aren't my concern."

You can respond:

*"I'm sorry you feel that way, but I would like for us to find
a way that the work can get done while still allowing me to
deal with my responsibilities at home. I'll agree to work
overtime this week, but I'd like to take off early a few days
next week."*

#5 "I'M OVERWORKED!"

If you find yourself overworked at the expense of your health,
family life, or general well-being, then it is a matter of survival
to inform your supervisor that you are working too many hours.
Make a chart showing all tasks you do in a typical week and the
approximate time each task takes. Give the list to your boss and
then say:

*"I know that completing all of these tasks is important, but
as you can see from my status report, they take between
fifty and sixty hours per week to complete."*

If your boss says:

*"I don't care how long they take you to finish—that's your
job and if you want to keep it, you'd better get them done!"*

You can respond:

*"Excuse me, Ms. Smith, but I am willing to put in some
overtime. However, I physically cannot continue to work
this number of hours every week. There's a limit, and I've
reached it."*

If your boss says:

> *"I don't know what you want me to do about it. The work has got to be done, and that's it!"*

You can respond:

> *"Ms. Smith, I see two options if you want the work to get done properly and on this highly pressured schedule."*

Your boss (now more open and interested since you have stood up for yourself) says:

> *"Oh, really, two options! What are they?"*

You can say calmly:

> *"Option one: You hire more skilled help to achieve your challenging production goals. Option two: You set new priorities for at least some of your existing workload."*

#6 "YOU'RE NEVER SATISFIED!"

Nothing is more discouraging than working your hardest yet never hearing your boss say, *"Good job!"* Little or no praise creates resentment, frustration, and a negative attitude that frequently lowers your productivity. Here are two tactful ways to encourage your boss to give you more praise and constructive feedback. Say:

> *"I don't mind having my mistakes pointed out so that I can correct them, but it also helps my work to know what I did right."*

If your boss responds:

> *"Look, I don't have time to hold your hand."*

You can respond:

> *"Ms. Anderson, I'm not asking you to 'hold my hand,' as you put it, but simply to approve what I do. Positive feedback along with constructive criticism helps me be more productive."*

#7 "QUIT TREATING ME LIKE A DOG!"

Some supervisors may bark orders, rudely snap at you for no reason, expect you to read their minds, or act in a nasty, unpleasant way. Rather than stomping off in a huff or passively accepting an abusive boss's vicious temper tantrum, take an assertive approach.

If your boss slams your recently completed assignment down on your desk and snarls:

"Is this what you call good work?"

You can respond:

"Please, let me see it for a moment. Just what seems to be the problem?"

If your boss now becomes more antagonistic and shouts:

"I can't believe you are asking me that! Any bozo would know what's wrong with this work! You've made a terrible mistake!"

You can respond:

"Excuse me, Mr. Johnson! I can see that you are upset, but I still expect to be treated with respect. If I made a mistake, I'll take responsibility for it. Apparently I don't understand what you want me to do. Please give me some specific examples, and I'll do it again."

If your boss continues to rant and rave:

"The agency said you were a top professional, but I've seen better work out of my parakeet!"

You can interrupt your boss by firmly saying:

"Now, wait a minute, Mr. Johnson! You have no right to talk to me in a way that shows a total disregard for my feelings. I know that you want things done in a certain way,

*and I'll correct any mistakes that I make, but I want you to
treat me with respect and common courtesy."*

In most cases when you stand up to an abusive boss, he or she
will back off at least temporarily. This may be a good time to
suggest:

*"Mr. Johnson, I think we need to improve our communi-
cation. Can we get together for a few minutes to come up
with a way of working together more efficiently?"*

#8 "STOP HARASSING ME, YOU PERVERT!"

Sexual harassment in the workplace is inappropriate and illegal.
While your boss's personal problems or poor judgment may be
the cause of his or her unprofessional conduct, inappropriate
sexual advances can make your life at work miserable.

Before you go over your boss's head to complain, make an
effort to address the problem by privately confronting your boss
with a short, prepared statement. Ask for a few minutes of
private time, look him or her in the eye, and say something like:

*"I want to make it perfectly clear that your sexual advances
and crude remarks are not welcome, and I want them to
stop."*

If your boss laughs it off and says:

*"Me make sexual advances and crude remarks? Ha! You
wish! Anyway, you office girls are too sensitive! Now, brush
away your tears, put a smile back on your pretty little face,
and get back to work."*

Respond by defining for your boss what constitutes sexual harassment. You can say something like:

*"Mr. Lane, in case you don't know, sexual remarks, un-
wanted invitations, suggestive pictures, intimidation, taunts,
leering, and patting or pinching are all forms of sexual harassment. If you don't stop harassing me, I'm going to lodge
a formal complaint with your boss, our company, my union,*

and the Equal Opportunity Commission in Washington!"
(The Equal Opportunity Commission offers assistance in
some sexual harassment cases. It is located at 1801 L St.
N.W., Washington, D.C. 20507. Telephone: 202-663-4264)

Before you make a formal oral or written complaint concerning
sexual harassment in the workplace, document each inappropriate incident, including the time, place, any witnesses, and a
brief nonjudgmental description of the person's words and actions. This is your ammunition if the abuse does not stop and
you need to present your case to a higher authority in the company. If you do file a complaint, make at least three copies of the
letter. Send one copy to the offending person, one copy to his or
her supervisor, and keep one copy for yourself.

Be prepared, however, for your boss's supervisor to downplay the problem and support your boss, unless there have been
other similar complaints. If this is the case, and if you want to
pursue the complaint, then you may want to contact your local
and national union representative, your company's personnel
or human-resources department, or the Equal Employment Opportunities Commission in your city, state, or in Washington,
D.C., for more information. In most cases, however, the most
effective way to deal with harassment in the workplace is to
extricate yourself from the harasser's influence as quickly as
possible.

#9 "I DEMAND A TRANSFER!"

Whether you request a transfer to advance your career or es-
cape an abusive boss, do your homework before you make an
official request. Informally talk to other employees about possible positions in your company. Ask other employees about a
department supervisor's reputation. Their response will help
you determine if your working styles are compatible. After all,
what good is trading one bad supervisor or department for
another? When you are ready, present your request for transfer
orally and in writing to the head of your division, not your
supervisor.

If you want a transfer because your present department offers little or no opportunity for advancement, you can say:

"I am requesting a transfer to the . . . department because I think I will have a better chance of fulfilling my career goals, which are to. . . . I've enjoyed working for you and I want to thank you for all your help and support."

If you want a transfer to another department because of a personal conflict or sexual harassment, briefly cite your reasons, but be prepared to back up any accusations you make with specific documented evidence. Keep in mind that you will increase your chances of success if you remain unemotional and say that your company stands to benefit from your transfer. For example, you can write something like the following to the head of your department:

(Date)

Department Head
XYZ Company
Bigtown, New York 10000

Dear Department Head:

I am requesting a transfer to another department because over the last two years I've had no opportunity for career advancement.

In this department I have been passed over for job openings that I am qualified to perform.

I have contributed a lot to the department since I began working for this company over two years ago, and I deserve to be judged for promotions based on my job performance. Therefore I believe I can make a greater contribution to the company if I am transferred to another department. Thank you for your understanding and consideration in this matter.

Sincerely,

(Your name)
(Your position)

#10 "I QUIT!"

Sometimes, after you've tried everything you can think of to solve a problem at work, you may decide that your only option is to quit your job. If you do decide to leave your job, you can do so in one of two ways—either gracefully or with drama and animosity. Your timing, choice of words, and preparation make all the difference in the world, even if you and your boss do not always see eye to eye.

Make it your goal to leave your job on friendly terms, because you never know when you may face your boss again, either at the same company or in a new position with another organization. Plus, news travels fast within industries. You don't want the reputation of being a person who is difficult to work with, even if the problems were not entirely your fault. To avoid a tense showdown and to increase your chances of receiving a letter of recommendation, follow these tips:

- Type a short, unemotional letter stating why you are resigning.
- Include the effective date. Two weeks is standard.
- Outline plans for an orderly transfer of responsibility.
- Offer your services if your successor has any questions.
- Make every effort to end the letter on a positive note by writing a few words of thanks to your boss for his or her help.

Your letter of resignation might read something like this:

(Date)

Ms. Mary Beethoven
The Grand Piano Company
1234 Piano Lane
Musicville, New York 12345

Dear Ms. Beethoven:

After a great deal of thought, I have decided to resign from my position as secretary with the Grand Piano Company to pursue other career opportunities. My last day of work will be. . . . Over the next two weeks I'll complete my last assignments and prepare my files for my replacement. Of course I will be happy to help the person taking over my responsibilities make the transition as smoothly as possible.

Deciding to leave the Grand Piano Company was a difficult decision because I've learned a tremendous amount while working in your department. I also want to take this opportunity to thank you for your help and support over the last two years.

Sincerely,

(Your name)

Ask to meet with your boss, preferably on Friday, at the end of a pay period, or after completing a major assignment. Say something like:

"I'd like to talk to you about an important matter. Could we get together for about ten minutes sometime today?"

Summarize what is in your letter of resignation, avoiding any negative comments, criticism, or parting shots—no matter how tempting they may be! After your boss has accepted your resignation and appears to be even mildly receptive or guilty for pushing you to this decision, consider asking him or her for a letter of recommendation. While he or she might say no, you've got nothing to lose by asking. Keep the tone of your voice upbeat, maintain steady eye contact and open body language, and smile, because you are on your way to a new adventure!

DEFINE YOUR CAREER GOALS AND PURSUE THEM— ONE DAY AT A TIME!

Rejections and unhappy work situations can be excellent motivators if you are willing to take action. If you feel you are in a dead-end job, then it is up to you to do something about it! Begin by writing down your long-term goals or "dream list"— and be as specific as possible! Where do you want to be living and what do you want to be doing in five years? How do you want to spend your time, earn your income, fulfill your needs? Next, make a plan that consists of about ten medium-term goals that will move you closer to your five-year goal. These intermediate goals will keep you on course. Finally, take immediate and steady action with short-term goals that move you closer to your dreams one day at a time.

CHAPTER 7

Tactful Ways to Tell the People You Supervise . . .

Are you a supervisor with this dilemma: You want to be well liked by your staff, but some of your subordinates mistake your friendliness as a signal that they can get away with shoddy work. To correct the situation, you must reprimand some workers, but you are afraid of alienating your staff and creating friction in your department.

This is just one of many difficult situations that managers find themselves in. After all, supervising would be easy if your department could accomplish all its production goals without you cracking the whip, reprimanding workers for wasting time, or making tough decisions without hurting someone's feelings. Being a motivator and monitor is part of a supervisor's job. If you combine assertiveness, flexibility, and sensitivity, your staff will respect your authority and be more open to your suggestions.

#11 "YOU TALK TOO MUCH!"

Chatterboxes can waste a lot of time at work. The following examples could take place in a private conference in your office or in public during a staff meeting. The goal is to check a subordinate's nonproductive behavior without humiliating him or her.

Here are some tactful approaches to bridling a blabbermouth:

The Office Socializer:

> *"Sandy, we appreciate your enthusiasm here, but lately I've noticed that you're spending a lot of time socializing. It really cuts your productivity and makes it hard for others in the office to concentrate on their work. I think it would be a big help to us all if you would focus more on your job and save your chatting for breaks or after work."*

The Long-winded Storyteller:

> *"Bill, I'm sure everyone wants to hear all the details of your fascinating fishing trip, but we are on a tight deadline and need to get down to business right now. Would you please save your story for lunch hour?"*

The Chronic Repeater:

> *"Jo, you've made an excellent point, but I think all of us understand that the problem is. . . . Now let's get to the solutions. What do you suggest as a first step?"*

The Conversation Dominator:

> *"Excuse me, Rick, sorry to interrupt. We appreciate your knowledge of the subject, but we'd like to hear some other opinions. Who's next to speak?"*

#12 "THIS ASSIGNMENT IS ALL WRONG!"

Everyone makes mistakes on the job. It takes a tactful supervisor to get workers to "do it again" without demoralizing them. If you only point out errors and neglect to credit parts of the job done correctly, you can discourage hardworking employees. So, when offering constructive criticism, first say what part of the job the person executed well. Let the praise sink in for a precious moment or two before you suggest specific changes or ask that the assignment be redone. Note the pause in these three examples:

"Rex, I'm pleased you caught our client's accounting mistake. You did a good job. (Pause) While I agree with you that their bookkeeping is sloppy, your letter sounds blunt and could be interpreted as arrogant. Insulting the client could cost us their account—and we certainly don't want that to happen! I'd like you to rewrite the letter more tactfully. Just ask them to please recalculate their figures to see if they agree with ours."

"Chan, you've come up with some terrific ideas that the sales reps will love. Good work! (Pause) After reading your plan over, I came up with some changes that will make it even better. I'd like to go over these with you now so that you can incorporate them into the plan by the end of the day."

"Diane, I can see you worked hard on this project. You certainly get an 'A' for effort. (Pause) However, my instructions may not have been clear, or you didn't understand how to do the task. Whichever is the case, the work needs to be done over. I want us to go over the job together so that you can get started on the right track. Between the two of us we'll get it right!"

#13 "THIS IS NOT WHAT I CALL NEAT WORK!"

Not every unsatisfactory job is the result of poor communication or lack of training. Sometimes people do poor quality work with the hope that it will slip by without comment. If you want to be a successful manager, never accept substandard work. Be direct but friendly when you return the work to your subordinate. Remind the person that you expect the work that he or she performs to meet or exceed certain standards, and make sure you clearly define those expectations. Privately tell the neglectful worker:

"Suzanne, I can't accept this work. There are a lot of problems. It's messy, filled with mistakes, and is going to cause

*extra work for the next person who works on it. I want to
remind you that all orders must be typed, not scribbled on
scrap paper. Also, I want you to double-check your work
and correct any errors before you pass it along to the accounting department. Any questions?"*

Don't be surprised if the subordinate acts a bit defensive or
mumbles something unintelligible when you return the assignment. He or she may say something like:

"I didn't have enough time!"

"There was no one here to help me!"

*"My other boss didn't care how it looked, as long as I did
the work."*

You can respond:

*"I know it's frustrating when good work is tossed back at
you, but let's face it, this is not good work. So, this time,
please do the job right. Do you have any questions?"*

In most cases you should see an improvement the next time
your worker turns in an assignment, but watch out that he or
she doesn't slip back into the old habit of doing substandard
work.

If a normally productive worker's performance slips drasti-
cally, you may need tactfully to ask a few personal questions to
help him or her resolve the problem. To open the discussion,
invite your subordinate into your office, close the door, and say
something like:

*"Carlos, I've noticed that the quality of your work has been
slipping steadily for the last few weeks, and it's hurting our
team's morale and productivity. I'm wondering, are you
having a problem that I might be able to help you with?"*

*"Jane, your sales have gone way down over the last couple
of months, and you're taking a lot of sick leave. I think
maybe we'd better talk about what's going on with you."*

Emphasize that you do not want to hear any personal details and are not offering advice—you just want to stop a personal problem before it becomes an unmanageable work problem. Say that all personal information is completely confidential. If your subordinate does reveal a personal or medical problem, you might suggest that he or she consult a health-care professional as soon as possible.

Keep in mind, however, that as a supervisor you may be responsible for frequent mistakes when your team members are:

- Working too fast to meet unreasonable deadlines.
- Overtired from working long hours.
- Too competitive with each other or not getting along.
- Situated in a poorly lighted or ventilated area.
- Using inadequate or poorly functioning equipment.

If you can identify any of these problems as a cause of frequent mistakes, then it is up to you, the supervisor, to find a solution by adjusting the workload, deadlines, teams, or work environment.

#14 "STOP FEUDING, OR I'LL FIRE BOTH OF YOU!"

What is the best way to deal with feuding subordinates? Taking sides may make one worker happy but will certainly alienate the other. On the other hand, ignoring staff problems with the hope that they will go away almost never works and often leads to more tension. However, if you get caught up in dealing with a lot of petty complaints, you'll waste time being a mediator instead of a manager. Rather than making one person feel defensive by stating an anonymous accusation, take an even-handed approach and identify the major conflicts by separately asking the parties involved for pertinent details. You can ask:

"Kim, I've noticed a lot of tension between you and Joe. In your view, what seems to be the problem?"

"Joe, you and Kim seem to be at odds. What exactly is the trouble?"

Then ask both parties into your office to make sure everyone agrees on the specific problem. Once you've established the facts, suggest a working compromise. For example, if the two workers are fighting over who uses the only available office computer, rephrase your perception of the problem. You can say:

> *"As I understand it, whoever gets on the computer first thing in the morning doesn't leave until late afternoon. As a result, the other person doesn't get to use the computer until late in the day. Is that right?"*

(Pause for both workers to agree that this is the source of the conflict.)

> *"In that case, I suggest we make a schedule so that both of you can use the computer and make your deadlines. How about this? Kim inputs her data in the morning and Joe inputs his data in the afternoon. You can alternate this schedule each week."*

(Pause for both workers to agree to this compromise.)

> *"I want to emphasize this point and make it absolutely clear to both of you. We're working on the same team, and I want this petty feuding to stop as of now. Agreed?"*

If, however, this kind of counterproductive competition persists, you may need to call both people into the office at the same time and present them with an ultimatum. You can say:

> *"Kim and Joe, please listen carefully. Your bickering is disrupting our work, and I can't allow that to continue. Take the next few minutes and get this problem resolved, or at least put it aside so that we can get back to work. This is the bottom line: If you two can't find a way of working together, then I may have to impose my own solution—which may not make either of you happy. So what's it going to be?"*

#15 "YOU'VE GOT A LOUSY ATTITUDE!"

Excessive complaints, sarcasm, backbiting, hostility, and low enthusiasm are just a few examples of a worker's poor attitude, but these symptoms also indirectly communicate dissatisfaction with your management style. When workers feel unappreciated or frustrated, their morale and productivity suffer—and so does the rest of your department. Instead of criticizing a worker's negative attitude, seek the underlying causes. Your objective is to change your worker's attitude by improving the situation. Listen carefully and nondefensively to what your worker has to say. You can ask:

> *"Alvarez, you seem kind of down lately, and I've noticed that you're not as enthusiastic about our project as usual. Can you tell me what's bothering you?"*

> *"Sophie, over the last couple of weeks I've noticed that you are making a lot of sarcastic remarks during our meetings. You are obviously upset about something. What's troubling you?"*

> *"Malcolm, you seem to be giving me the 'silent treatment.' I know you're angry about something. How about leveling with me? What's the problem?"*

Unhappy workers may shout, cry, walk away, or clam up when they are angry. This presents a manager with an extremely challenging and often delicate situation. Here are some tips for dealing with a highly agitated subordinate:

- Do not react to anything he or she says. Simply listen.
- Try not to get defensive if the worker criticizes you or your management style. Remember, a subordinate's honest feedback can help you become a more effective manager.
- If the worker starts yelling or crying, remain calm and resist the temptation to shout back.
- Give your subordinate a chance to calm down by suggesting that you both take a short break and talk again a little later.
- If the worker walks away or clams up, never use force to make him or her stay or talk. Rather, say you'd like to com-

plete the discussion so that you can both put the problem behind you.

While many supervisors only criticize their subordinates' work, a smart manager knows that even the best workers need to be praised. Praising the people who work for you eliminates resentment and shows that you appreciate their creativity, hard work, productivity, and accomplishments. Some people feel uncomfortable when they are praised by others. To ease their embarrassment, follow your positive comment with a short, easy-to-answer question.

Here are some examples of praise followed by an easy-to-answer question:

> *"Greg, you did a terrific job designing that book cover. What gave you the idea of using that theme in the first place?"*

> *"Celia, I really appreciate the way you handled that angry customer. I thought she was going to blow her stack, but you quieted her right down. How did you do it?"*

> *"Your presentation was absolutely terrific. Where did you learn how to talk like that?"*

#16 "I'M BREAKING MY PROMISE TO YOU."

There's a lot of truth in the saying "Don't make promises you can't keep." Sometimes even good supervisors make promises only to renege on them at a later date. While going back on your word is embarrassing, the sooner you correct your blunder, the better. Explain your mistake, apologize, and don't blame others for your goof. If possible, offer a compromise. For example:

> *"Ellen, I made a mistake when I promised you Ian's office. I should have sent your request to the personnel department. I'll put in a good word for you, but I'm afraid it's their decision. I apologize for making a promise I couldn't keep."*

"Tom, I'm sorry to have to tell you this, but I completely goofed up when I promised you next Friday off. I forgot that our team has to make a presentation to the sales staff that day, and we need everyone there to demonstrate the materials. What other day would you be willing to take off?"

"Ed, it was wrong of me to promise you Ann's old job after she gets her promotion. I apologize. I'll give you a good recommendation, but you'll have to interview for the position like the other candidates."

#17 "YOU'RE NOT GETTING A PROMOTION."

Denying a subordinate a promotion can cause hard feelings. If you avoid giving constructive suggestions or merely say that a more qualified candidate got the job, your worker will not know how to improve. Plus, he or she will probably feel frustrated and may have little hope of ever getting promoted. You can soften your worker's disappointment and help increase his or her chances of future advancement if you say:

"Dean, thanks for applying for the position of . . . , but you need to gain more experience in . . . and increase your skills at. . . ."

If your subordinate responds:

"This isn't fair. I never get any breaks!"

You can respond:

"Dean, when you improve your . . . skills, then you'll have a better chance of getting the job when a similar position opens up. I suggest that you seriously consider taking the training course we discussed. You've got to do some work, but it will pay off for you in the future."

#18 "I'M NOT RAISING YOUR PAY ONE NICKEL!"

Most salaries are tied to performance reviews and promotions. However, when a worker requests an unscheduled raise, a manager must often say no. A manager must be firm and fair, yet encouraging when rejecting a worker's plea for more money, otherwise the worker will certainly feel discouraged. Offer realistic and helpful suggestions so that the worker has incentive to improve his or her performance and hopefully be granted a raise in the not-too-distant future. For example, you can say:

> *"Elise, I'm afraid I'm going to have to deny your special request for a raise because at this time your overall job performance doesn't warrant it."*

If your subordinate responds:

> *"I don't get it, Jackie and I do the same job and she gets a dollar more an hour than I do. It's not right!"*

You can respond:

> *"Elise, if you performed your job as well as Jackie does, then I'd recommend that you receive a raise, but the quality of your work is not yet up to that level."*

Your subordinate groans:

> *"Oh, I give up!"*

You can respond:

> *"Look, Elise, I know you're frustrated, but I don't want you to give up. If you want a raise, you have to be more productive, and I'm willing to help you. Let's take a look at your performance reviews and pinpoint the areas where you can improve so that in a few months' time when you ask again, I can say yes."*

Frequently a manager must deny a request for a raise because of budget constraints. When this is the case, you can say something like:

> *"Josie, even though you deserve a raise, I simply haven't got the money in my budget. You'll just have to wait until your annual review. I'm sorry, but there's nothing else I can do."*

If an employee has reached the top of his or her salary level, you can say:

> *"Jim, you're at the top step of your classification, so I can't increase your salary. I suggest that if you want more money, you keep your eye open for a higher-level job with more responsibility and opportunity for advancement."*

If your subordinate responds:

> *"Oh, that's really disappointing! You know how much I like working in this department! Isn't there anything you can do?"*

You can respond:

> *"Other than give you a great recommendation, I'm afraid that's about it."*

If a wage freeze affects your entire staff, then make the announcement to the group and be sympathetic. You can say,

> *"I'm sorry to have to tell everyone this, but I'm the messenger who is bearing some bad news. Our company has found it necessary to freeze all wages until further notice. I know this is bad news for all of us here—myself included—and I'm not going to try to convince you otherwise."*

If your subordinates respond:

> *"We're barely getting by as it is! What are we supposed to do?"*

You can reassure them by saying:

> *"I know it's tough making ends meet. Business is bad and the company is having the same problem. The fact is, if this place goes out of business, we'll all be out of a job. When the situation changes, I'm sure that your normal increases will be reinstated."*

#19 "WE'RE ELIMINATING YOUR JOBS."

When executives toss around words like *downsizing, rightsizing, pink slips,* and *compensation packages,* supervisors and managers are usually the ones chosen to dole out the bad news to the staff. If laying off workers becomes part of your responsibilities, tell each person as early as possible in the privacy of your office. Emphasize that the decision was difficult and that it was not the worker's fault. Your objective is to minimize the sting of the decision, offer support and sympathy, and help in the transition. Even though most workers realize that the decision may not be entirely yours, be prepared for angry reactions, disbelief, and resentment. It is best to be direct but sympathetic and have information about unemployment insurance and outplacement. Here's what you can say:

> *"Anna, I'm sorry, but we have to lay you off. I just want you to know that your work has been fine, but due to circumstances in the marketplace, we need to let some people go."*

If she responds:

> *"How can you do this to me after all I've done for this company? I can't believe it!"*

You can say:

> *"I understand that this news is upsetting, but there is nothing I can do to change it. I'm sorry, because I liked working with you and I think your work is excellent."*

If your subordinate says:

"A lot of good that does me! What am I going to do for money? I've got bills to pay!"

You can respond:

"Believe me, I wish I didn't have to do this. I have gathered some information for you about obtaining unemployment insurance and other benefits that may be helpful. I'll write you a letter of recommendation and ask some of my colleagues if they know of any openings. I can't promise you anything, but if the situation changes here and we need people again, I'd like to call you back to work."

#20 "YOU'RE FIRED!"

For most managers, firing an employee is the most unpleasant task they face in their jobs. As a manager, you must consider the worker's rights under the law as well as his or her feelings. Before you terminate an employee, it is wise to check your company's policy. Here is an accepted step-by-step disciplinary method:

1. A documented oral reprimand.
2. Specific guidance to correct the problem.
3. A written warning specifying the problem and the time allowed for its elimination.
4. An employee hearing to allow the employee an opportunity to tell his or her side of the story.
5. A one-day suspension to show that the problem remains.
6. A last warning to tell the employee that if his or her behavior does not change within a given period of time, termination is likely.
7. An exit interview to explain the reason for being terminated.

Your goal is to sever the relationship between the employee and your company in a civil manner, allowing him or her to remain dignified and not feel that your decision was abrupt or unfair. Once again, when you deliver bad news, be prepared for crying, shouting, walking away, or other emotional outbursts. Remain calm, professional, and as sympathetic as the situation allows. Here's what you can say:

> *"Pat, we're letting you go. Over the past several weeks I've tried to explain to you the problems that you needed to correct, but I've seen no changes."*

Or you can say:

> *"Pat, after careful consideration we've concluded that your job here isn't working out. I'd like to suggest a mutual agreement that we part ways."*

Then, without debating the issue or waffling on your decision, go on to say:

> *"Today is your last day, but it is our company's policy to give you two weeks' severance pay. Also, here is some written information about benefits that you may be eligible for while you look for other work."*

Finally, allow the terminated worker to respond to your decision and listen for his or her reaction, but don't rescind your decision. Then end the final interview by:

- Highlighting any achievements or personal attributes the employee had while working for you.
- Coming to an agreement about what will be said to prospective employers.
- If the discussion ends on professional terms, offering the employee a handshake.

PRODUCTIVE SUPERVISORS ARE TACTFUL

Today's highly demanding workplace requires you, as a supervisor, to know how to get the most from your staff while at the same time treating them with the respect and appreciation they want and deserve. Tactful communication is one of the most important tools you can use to supervise any group of workers effectively. A simple golden rule applies here:

Treat and talk to your staff in the same way that you want them to treat and talk to you.

DOS AND DON'TS FOR SUPERVISORS

Do make your comments and corrections specific.
Don't be vague and wishy-washy.
Do treat everyone fairly and with respect.
Don't play favorites.
Do preface constructive criticism with praise.
Don't just focus on the mistakes.
Do offer more praise than criticism to your subordinates.
Don't chide an employee in the presence of other co-workers.
Do remain friendly and enthusiastic.
Don't be angry when your subordinates make mistakes.
Do solicit ways that the person can change or improve.
Don't talk like a benevolent dictator or condescending parent.
Do remain friendly after a reprimand.
Don't avoid confronting hard-to-handle subordinates.
Do ask questions to make sure your staff knows what you expect.
Don't assume that your directions are as clear as a bell.
Do avoid controversial subjects with your staff.
Don't discuss your personal problems with your subordinates.
Do use your sense of humor to make your staff feel comfortable.
Don't gossip with coworkers about their peers.
Do let your workers know that you are available for questions.
Don't forget that making small talk with your staff shows that you care about the important matters in their lives.
Do say positive things about your staff in front of their co-workers.

CHAPTER 8

Tactful Ways to Tell Your Coworkers . . .

Does a coworker's cigarette smoke endlessly drift into your work area, causing you to gasp and wheeze? Is the new office assistant forever interrupting you for help with tasks that he could do on his own? Has your best office friendship degenerated into hostile competition? Do pushy coworkers invite you to social functions that you'd rather avoid?

Everyone faces difficult situations like these with coworkers at one time or another. Successfully handling on-the-job conflicts requires you to solve the specific problem without leaving you or your coworker feeling angry or hurt. If you let a troubling situation fester until you blow up, your coworker will be confused and resentful. On the other hand, if you say or do nothing about a problem, *you* may end up hostile and frustrated. Studies show that workers who assertively cope with the many interpersonal conflicts that come up on the job are most likely to succeed and advance in their careers. *Avoid* emotionally charged statements such as:

"You always . . ."

"Why can't you . . ."

"You should know better than to . . ."

"Why don't you. . . !"

Accusing comments like these usually aggravate the situation and make people hostile and uncooperative. While most people will gracefully comply to a reasonable request, a dictatorial demand made in a superior manner often yields the opposite results.

#21 "NOT AN INVITATION TO ANOTHER BORING PARTY!"

Have you ever been invited to a get-together after work at a local bar or coworker's home that you'd rather not attend? Maybe some of your coworkers tend to overindulge, get rowdy, or gossip with your boss or other coworkers. You may not want to attend a work-related social function, but refusing the invitation may cause hard feelings with your coworkers.

The next time you find yourself in this predicament, use this tactful three-step method to decline the invitation:

- First, rephrase the invitation to give yourself a few extra seconds to collect your thoughts.
- Second, give a polite refusal. You don't need to offer any specific reason for not attending, unless you happen to have a good excuse ready—which is not a bad idea!
- Finally, thank the person for the invitation.

Here are two tactful ways to decline an invitation:

"You're having a little get-together after work at Sam's Lounge? I'm sorry, I can't make it, but thanks for thinking of me."

"You say there's a party Friday night after work at Helen's apartment? Hmmm, let me check my calendar. I think I've already made plans, but thanks for inviting me."

Keep in mind that if you refuse every invitation to a work-related social function, it won't take your coworkers long to conclude that you don't like parties and don't want to socialize with them. To avoid negative feelings, consider accepting the invitation with a time limitation. You can say,

"You're having a party? I'd love to come, but I'll only be able to stay for about an hour or so. Thanks for the invitation!"

In this way you can socialize with your peers outside the workplace and know that you can gracefully leave the get-together before the situation becomes uncomfortable for you.

#22 "YOUR CONSTANT JABBERING DRIVES ME CRAZY!"

Prolonged loud talking in the office or frequent personal telephone calls can be an annoying problem among coworkers sharing an office space. Suppose several people often gather near your desk to chatter endlessly without regard to those working around them. Your chances of persuading loud coworkers to talk elsewhere will increase if you approach them in a friendly, but matter-of-fact manner. First try a light approach, by saying something like,

"Excuse me, folks. Sorry to interrupt 'Monday Morning at the Movies,' but I'm having trouble concentrating on this work because your voices carry so easily in here."

If someone sarcastically replies:

"What's wrong, don't you like movies?"

You can respond:

"Actually I love talking about movies, but if I don't get this report done by lunchtime, I'll be in hot water with my boss. Would you mind keeping your voices down, or better yet, move into the lounge or cafeteria?"

If a problem with a chatty coworker persists, ask the person for a minute of his or her time to explain the problem again. You can say:

"John, I don't want to make a big deal about this, but when your friends gather around your desk to socialize, it makes it hard for me to hear while I'm on the phone with clients."

If your fun-loving coworker replies:

"Oh, come on, lighten up. We're just having a little fun!"

You can respond:

"I'm sure you are, but it got so loud yesterday when I was on the telephone that one client asked me if we were having a tailgate party. If our boss heard that, he'd hit the roof! I'd appreciate it if you could remember that both of us have to share this work space."

If other people in your work area feel the same way you do about a coworker's loud talking, you can serve as a spokesperson and say,

"Vivian, you probably aren't aware of this, but when you talk on the telephone, your voice really carries throughout the office. I figured you would want to know because I'm sure you don't want everyone to overhear your personal business."

#23 I'M NOT YOUR PERSONAL ANSWERING SERVICE!

Does your gabby office mate receive so many personal calls that you end up being his or her answering service or else you have to listen to the phone ring endlessly? If so, you can curtail this annoying problem by following one or both of these examples:

You can say something like:

"Sam, I don't mind taking an occasional message for you, but I have a hard time finishing my work when your friends constantly call you and you aren't here to answer the phone."

If your talkative coworker answers:

"Well, what do you want me to do about it? I can't control who calls me!"

You can respond:

> *"Well, actually you can if you ask your friends to call you at home or leave messages with the receptionist."*

Say this to a coworker whose phone constantly rings:

> *"Charlene, when people call when you are away from your desk, they just let the phone ring off the hook. I either suffer through minutes of ringing or stop what I'm doing to take messages from your friends. I'd appreciate it if you would tell your friends to let the phone ring only two or three times and if you don't answer, then hang up and call you later or at home."*

#24 "YOUR CIGARETTE SMOKE STINKS!"

Smoking coworkers can be a hazard to your health. In many offices you are within your rights to ask a coworker to refrain from lighting up, and most will comply if you make the request politely. Even if "no smoking" is not an office policy, you can still say,

> *"Mike, when you smoke at your desk, your cigarette smoke drifts into my area and makes me sneeze like crazy. Would you mind going outside or to the smoking lounge to have a cigarette?"*

If the coworker snorts:

> *"I can't stop what I'm doing each time I want a cigarette. I'd never get anything done! Does it bother you that much?"*

You can respond:

> *"Yes, it does. Whenever you light a cigarette in our office, I have to leave, and that cuts into my productivity. I would really appreciate it if you would smoke in the designated smoking area."*

#25 "QUIT GRIPING ABOUT OUR BOSS!"

Coworkers complaining about their bosses are about as common as fleas on a junkyard dog. Even if it is tempting to join gripe sessions about a less-than-perfect supervisor, indiscreet comments frequently find their way to your boss's office—and can cause you embarrassment or even cost you a promotion! Rather than jumping on the boss-bashing bandwagon, listen more and talk less. Avoid complaints and offer ideas to improve the working situation. You can say something like:

"Our boss certainly has a different management style, but complaining isn't going to make him change. Maybe we can come up with a strategy that will help us deal with him more efficiently."

If your coworker responds:

"Why bother, he won't listen to anyone anyway!"

You can reply:

"You're probably right, but maybe he would be happy to see that his staff is willing to find ways to be more productive. I don't see any harm in trying to help."

If your coworker gives you a sly look and says:

"What are you trying to do, get a promotion? Do you know what he did last week? You wouldn't believe it, but . . ."

You can interrupt and say:

"Hold it, Ken, if you are not willing to do something to help improve things, what is complaining going to accomplish? I think it is a waste of time and energy. What do you think would improve the situation?"

#26 "KEEP YOUR HANDS OFF MY DESK!"

Have you ever misplaced an important manuscript, file, or document only to discover that a thoughtless coworker borrowed it and neglected to tell you? Many workers need to share files, computer disks, tools, or other important items, but if someone with whom you work frequently borrows things from you without asking or letting you know, you can say:

> *"Scott, I'm incredibly frustrated because I just spent over a half hour looking for these client files that were on my desk when I left. And now I find them on your desk!"*

If your coworker snaps:

> *"The client's files don't belong to you, they belong to the company, and I needed them. So what if I took them off your desk?*

You can respond:

> *"I don't have a problem with sharing the files with you or anyone else. Since I'm responsible for the files, I do have a problem when I don't know who is using them."*

If your coworker starts to argue and say:

> *"Okay, so I forgot to return them to you. I don't understand why you are making such a big deal about it."*

You can respond:

> *"Let me explain it to you. When I have to track them down, it wastes my time and makes extra work for me. So, please do me two favors. First, leave me a note if you take the client files, or anything else for that matter, off my desk. And second, whatever you borrow, please return it after you are through with it."*

#27 "I CAN'T DO MY JOB AND YOUR JOB TOO!"

Are you frequently interrupted by coworkers asking you for favors or help because they are too lazy or insecure to do the job themselves? A dependent coworker can sap your energy, goodwill, and productivity. Whether he or she is inexperienced, incompetent, or uncertain, the clinging coworker will make you feel more like a baby-sitter than a professional. The problem can become so acute that you may end up doing double work and be reprimanded by your boss for neglecting your own responsibilities.

One way out of this dilemma is to set clear limits as to how much you are willing to help the other person. Let the dependent coworker know that you do not have an endless amount of time to help but that you do sympathize with his problems. Impress upon him that in the end he, and not you, is responsible for his success or failure on the job. You can offer support and encouragement to a dependent coworker, but emphasize that you will not always be available to help him do the job. Begin with a warm smile, the person's first name, and say something like,

> *"Jill, I'm feeling a bit pressured this morning, so you'll have to carry on today without my help."*

If your coworker protests:

> *"Are you kidding? I'll never be able to do this work by myself! There's so much I don't understand and you're so good at it."*

You can respond:

> *"I understand that you feel overwhelmed in your new position, and that's natural, but you'll be a pro in no time. The more you do it, the better you will become."*

If the dependent coworker pleads:

> *"I just know I'm going to mess up, and when the boss finds out I can't do the work, he'll throw me out. Please, you've got to help me, just this once! Please?"*

You can make your limits clear by saying:

> *"Jill, I'm getting frustrated because I can't get my own work done when you ask me for help every few minutes. I am willing to help you when I can, but it's up to you to learn what is necessary to do the job properly. I'm sorry, but like I said, I won't be able to help you now."*

If you are willing to offer some help or suggestions, do so at your convenience. Here are three ways to tell the dependent coworker what you are willing to do for him or her:

> *"I may have a few minutes after lunch to give you some quick feedback on your work before you hand it in to your boss."*

> *"I found this part of the job difficult too. I made it easier by doing it one step at a time. If you're really having problems with doing the work, perhaps you can ask our boss to get you more training."*

> *"Have you considered taking a night class in typing (word processing, computers, etc.) to help make your job easier? I took a crash course in . . . , and it made all the difference in the world."*

#28 "I'M NOT GOING TO LIE FOR YOU!"

Do you have a coworker who always stretches the truth whenever your supervisor comes around and then asks you to back his excuse about why a job did not get done? These manipulators are always on the lookout for "soft touch" coworkers to save them from the boss's wrath. They don't want to pull their fair share at work. These people not only create problems, they are a problem! If a deceitful coworker asks you to just play along and back him or her up in a lie, be assertive and simply say:

> *"No, I don't feel comfortable lying to our boss. This job means too much to me to risk doing something foolish like that."*

If your slippery coworker tries to pressure you by saying:

"Our boss will never find out. Besides, you'll want me to cover for you sometime. Come on, it's no big deal!"

You can remain firm by saying:

"You'll have to handle this problem without my help."

If your coworker persists, use the broken-record strategy and repeat your answer. You can say:

"I guess you weren't listening. The answer is no."

#29 "YOU'RE NOT MY SUPERVISOR, SO DON'T BOSS ME AROUND!"

It's amazing how many Steamroller-type peers there are in the workplace! If you listen to these domineering despots, you'd think they were master sergeants in the army: *"Do this! Get that! Hurry up! I've got to have it now!"* The tyrannical coworker is truly offensive, because he or she orders you around like a subordinate, but doesn't have the authority to do so. You can stop a bossy coworker before he or she establishes a false sense of authority if you speak directly to him or her in a calm and assertive voice. At a quiet moment before work and out of earshot of other coworkers you can say something like this:

"Tina, maybe you have been working here longer than me, but I'm not your assistant. Would you mind asking someone else to make copies for you?"

If your pushy coworker explodes:

"Well, excuse me! I always have to do everything myself and I can see that you're not going to be much help around here!"

You can respond:

"Please, let me explain. I can see you are overworked, and I don't mind helping you. The thing is, we both have the

same position with the company, and I expect to be treated
as an equal and not as your helper."

#30 "STOP PLAYING YOUR COMPETITIVE GAMES."

You've probably met the overcompetitive coworkers who approach the workplace like a World Series play-off in which
there's always a winner and a loser. They consistently challenge
you to "see who's the best" at even the most trivial of tasks. This
friendly competition is often a way for bored workers to add a
little excitement to a mundane job. What begins as friendly
competition, however, can sometimes escalate into a tense working situation.

Do you and a coworker aggressively tease or taunt each other?
Are both of you highly secretive about your business activities,
or in extreme cases are you unfriendly, uncooperative, or out-
wardly hostile with each other? If this describes your working
relationship with a peer, then you'll need all the conversation
skills you can muster to stop what can be a job-threatening
confrontation. Here are some ways to tell competitive coworkers that you don't want to play this win-lose game:

"I don't want to make my job into a game. Let's just work
together and get the job done."

Your coworker may challenge you again by saying that competition brings out the best in everyone and that you're just afraid
to lose. Just stay cool and repeat your intention not to compete.
You can say:

"I guess I didn't make myself clear. I'm not worried about
who is the fastest at filing reports. I just do the best job I
can. Plus, I don't think competition creates a good working
relationship."

If your coworker challenges you with:

"Why not, what are you afraid of?"

You can answer:

"It makes me feel uncomfortable. If you are so determined to win all the time, why don't you move to the sales department and try to beat our competitors instead of the people on your own team?"

Here are some more examples of what to say to typical challenges by an overcompetitive coworker. If your coworker says:

"Let's bet a hundred bucks on who makes the most sales this month."

You can say:

"I have a better suggestion. Let's pool our efforts and aim to double our combined sales. That way we both win!"

If your coworker says:

"Let's both ask for a raise and see who gets it."

You can say:

"No. I'll ask for a raise when I think the time is best for me."

If your coworker says:

"Competition brings out the best in me because I love to win."

You can say:

"I don't take competition that seriously. I think it's destructive to office relationships."

If your coworker says:

"Whoever wins the Jones contract is the best salesperson."

You can say:

"We are both professionals and good at what we do. We don't need to prove anything to each other."

#31 "I'M NOT A MIND READER!"

Does a coworker snap at you, cause scenes, or unfairly criticize you? If so, then trouble may be brewing, and the sooner you uncover the problem between you, the better. Tension between coworkers is often an indirect expression of anger. By asking the right questions and listening actively for key words and hidden issues, you can define obstacles and find possible solutions to office conflicts. It is vital to defuse hostility before it escalates and ruins your office relationships.

When tension between you and your coworker becomes unbearable, you may wish to hold out an "olive branch" by suggesting that the two of you chat for a minute or two in private. By taking the initiative, you can help avoid a nasty scene. You might say something like:

"Fran, can we talk alone for a few minutes? It's obvious you are upset with me about something, and I'm not happy about our working relationship either. I'd like to talk it out. What do you say?"

If your surly coworker bluntly says:

"I don't think we have anything to talk about."

You can be persistent and say:

"Well, I think we do have something to talk about because whenever I see you, all I get is the cold shoulder. To be honest, working with you right now makes me feel kind of tense."

If your sarcastic coworker gives you a thin smile and says:

"Gee, that's too bad. I don't know what you want me to say."

You can press the issue by saying:

"I know it might be hard to talk about things that make you angry, but we need to work things out because our jobs depend on it. When would be a good time to get together and talk? How about after work tonight over a cup of coffee?"

Once your coworker agrees to talk, find a quiet and private place. Admit any mistakes that you have made, but emphasize that you want to get your relationship back on track. You can say:

"I admit that I may have been too pushy when I started this job. Sometimes I let my enthusiasm carry me away. I apologize if I came on a bit strong. I'd like to give it a fresh start. What do you say?"

You don't have to explain or apologize too much. Let your apology stand alone, even if it means an uneasy silence between the two of you. Your coworker is very likely considering how sincere you are and how she is going to respond. Hopefully, she will express a mutual desire to find a better way to communicate. Suggest that the two of you brainstorm to come up with a few specific changes in the way you work together. You can say:

"Maybe we can think of ways we can improve the way we work together. I think one thing that would help is to talk more about what each of us is doing. How about meeting for a few minutes each morning to discuss our daily agenda in more detail and see if we can work out the kinks before they become a problem?"

If all else fails and your coworker remains hostile, you can say in a matter-of-fact way:

"We both have a lot to lose if we can't work out this problem—it could cost us our jobs! We don't have to be great friends, but at this point we do have to work together, so let's try to get along as best we can."

#32 "STOP TALKING BEHIND MY BACK!"

While gossip is part of life in the workplace, being the target of a malicious rumor can ruin your career! Stopping a gossiping coworker requires an assertive statement such as *"Stop spreading rumors about me!"* Before you confront the rumormonger, write out *exactly* what you want to say. Be brief and polite. Find a private place to meet, take a deep breath, and talk to the troublemaker face-to-face. In a calm and firm voice say:

> *"I'm upset because I've heard that you are spreading rumors about me. That bothers me because it makes my work more difficult and jeopardizes my job. You can think whatever you please, but please stop gossiping about me."*

If the gossiping coworker pleads innocent by saying:

> *"I don't know what you're talking about. Someone has been telling you lies! I've never said a bad word about you!"*

Respond to the gossip's denials by clarifying the situation and separating truth from rumor. You can say:

> *"I appreciate that you would never say a bad word about me. I know that people are saying. . . . The facts are. . . ."*

If you do not want to reveal any information, and want to set the rumormonger straight, you can say in no uncertain terms:

> *"I know you have been gossiping about me because several friends of mine told me so! Do me a favor, just stay out of my business."*

Politely end the conversation with a clear message that you can forgive and forget the coworker's indiscretion, but that you expect the gossiping to stop. You can say:

> *"I hope I've cleared up any misconceptions that you may have. As far as I'm concerned, I want to get on with our job here and keep my personal life out of it! Is that okay with you?"*

Office gossips thrive on secrecy, distortion, and repeating comments out of context. Your best defense against being the target of a career-damaging rumor is to keep your personal life out of the workplace and to resolve any misunderstandings or unsettled issues between you and your coworkers quickly and quietly.

DOS AND DON'TS FOR BETTER CONVERSATIONS WITH COWORKERS

Do make an effort to show a personal interest in your coworkers.

Don't gossip about or bad-mouth your coworkers.

Do cooperate with your coworkers to build more productive teams.

Don't compete with your coworkers, because it causes resentment.

Do make an effort to mend fences and resolve outstanding issues.

Don't assume that problems with coworkers will go away by themselves.

Do solicit input from your coworkers to improve your productivity.

Don't be a know-it-all.

Do compliment your coworkers' talents, hard work, and good ideas.

Don't pass by an opportunity to help a coworker in a crunch.

CHAPTER 9

Tactful Ways to Tell Sales and Business Associates . . .

Do phone solicitors call and interrupt your dinner hour with high-pressured sales pitches? Do volunteers pester you for more contributions, even though you've already sent their organization a check? Do you suffer through poorly prepared restaurant meals that ought to be sent back to the kitchen? Do you hesitate to tell your lawyer, accountant, or doctor that you are disappointed with his or her services? Do contractors tell you one price, then charge you more, and leave a mess for you to clean up? Do pushy salespeople manipulate you into keeping defective merchandise?

Everyone faces insults and assaults from the world of commerce. The question is, how do you tell sales and business people what you want—or don't want—without losing your temper? Communicating with tact allows you to retain your composure, guide the conversation, resolve conflict, and achieve your desired results. Plus, dealing assertively with sales and business people does wonders for your confidence and self-esteem!

#33 "I DON'T WANT TO BUY ANYTHING!"

It's six-fifteen P.M. and you've just sat down to spend a precious hour with your family over dinner. As you take your first bite, the telephone rings. You worry that it's your mother, best friend, or someone with an emergency, so you answer the telephone only to hear an unfamiliar voice asking:

> *"Hello, is this Mr. or Mrs. (they always pronounce your name wrong!)? I'm from the Widget Home Improvement Company and I want to tell you about our special rate on replacement siding for homes in your neighborhood. Are you interested?"*

After a resounding no, you slam the telephone down and march back to the dinner table in a huff, ranting and raving about how salespeople always call during dinnertime. Now you're aggravated, and what began as a pleasant meal has been disrupted.

A tactful rejection will quickly end a sales call without spoiling your mood. The sooner the phone solicitor finds that you are not a good prospect, the better it is for both of you. Don't let him or her talk for more than ten seconds before politely interrupting and saying:

> *"Excuse, me, but I'm not interested in your offer. Good-bye."*

If the persistent salesperson continues with a hard-selling pitch, such as:

> *"You'll be sorry if you pass up an offer as good as this! It will only take me ninety seconds to explain how you can save over five hundred dollars on new siding if you order a free estimate right now."*

You can interrupt again and say:

> *"I said I'm not interested and I don't appreciate being called at the dinner hour. Please take my name off your calling list. Thank you. Good-bye."*

Then gently hang up the telephone with the knowledge that the interruption had a minimal impact on your life. Another variation for ending an unwanted telephone sales call is to say:

"I don't want to waste your time or mine; I'm not inter-ested. Please take my name off your calling list. Thank you. Good-bye."

If you are interested in hearing more about the offer, but the sales call comes at an inconvenient time, interrupt the salesper-son and say:

"I'm sorry to interrupt you, but I can't talk now. I'd like to hear more about your offer. Please call me back at. . . . Then I'll have a few minutes to listen. Thanks. Good-bye."

#34 "I'M NOT CONTRIBUTING ANY MORE MONEY."

Every charity wants money, and there is no shortage of worthy causes to support. The problem is that just when the ink is barely dry on a check to your favorite charity, another crusader calls and asks for a donation. Rejecting the plight of suffering animals, the homeless, and other hapless individuals is difficult. Unless you have unlimited funds, you are sure to face financial ruin if you feel compelled to give money to every organization that asks you for it. Here are some surefire ways to politely reject people who solicit charitable contributions. You can say:

"I've just recently made a donation to your organization, and that's all I can afford to give right now."

If the volunteer pressures you for more by saying:

"I see you only gave twenty-five dollars this last year. Our organization does so many good things. Can't you help us out with a fifty-dollar donation?"

You can respond:

"I think your organization is doing a fine job, but twenty-five dollars is all I can contribute for now. Keep up the good work. Good-bye!"

If the person attempts to manipulate you with a guilt-provoking pitch, such as:

"If you don't help us, many innocent animals will continue to suffer. Won't you please open your heart and make a small gift? It really is a good cause!"

Even if you feel like caving in, be assertive and say:

"I'm sorry. But the answer is no. Good-bye."

If you want to end frequent calls for charitable contributions from a particular organization, ask to speak to the supervisor and say:

"I'm not making any more contributions to your organization. Please remove my name and telephone number from your calling list. Thank you."

#35 "THIS MEAL IS UNACCEPTABLE!"

Has this aggravating situation ever happened to you? You have a special evening to celebrate and you've made reservations at an expensive restaurant for you and your companion. Much to your chagrin, you wait forty-five minutes and then get seated near the kitchen. To make matters worse, it takes your surly waiter another twenty minutes to ask for your order. When your meals finally come, your companion's steak is burned instead of rare and the accompanying string beans are ice cold.

Dining out is supposed to be a pleasurable experience, but nothing can leave a bad taste in your mouth faster than receiving a poorly prepared meal—and then paying a large bill! Unfortunately yelling at the waiter or throwing a tantrum in public will only embarrass your companion and ruin your special evening.

Getting Poor Table Service? Ask to See the Manager

Conscientious restaurant managers want to know if their patrons are unhappy with meals because they understand that dissatisfied customers do not come back or recommend their eating establishment to others. Correcting an unacceptable meal improves a restaurant's reputation because patrons know that the management cares about their customers and values their business.

Here are some acceptable ways of dealing with an unacceptable meal and poor table service. Once again, tact and assertiveness are your tools to correct the problem without getting upset or causing an embarrassing situation. Immediately call the waiter to your table. If he or she is nowhere to be seen, politely ask any other waiter or person employed by the restaurant to pass this message along by saying:

"Excuse me. Will you ask our waiter to come to our table immediately? There is a problem with our meal. Thank you."

When your waiter appears, simply say:

"We have a problem with this meal. I ordered . . . , and as you can see, that's not what we have received. I'd appreciate it if you would please bring me. . . . Thank you."

If the waiter begins to argue with you by saying:

"You ordered your meat well done, not rare. I can handle this job, believe me. I'm a college graduate!"

Don't bother discussing the matter with your waiter any further. Politely ask to see the manager immediately. When the manager arrives, say:

"I'm sure you and your chef want to know when a meal isn't prepared or presented correctly. I tried explaining the problem with our meal to our waiter, but he doesn't seem to understand. Will you please tell the chef that we want this meat cooked rare. Thank you."

A smart restaurant manager will quickly correct the problem and explain to the waiter how to handle customers who are dissatisfied with a meal. If the manager isn't helpful, you can say:

"I'm taking my business elsewhere."

#36 "YOU BROKE IT—YOU FIX IT!"

After paying for an expensive engine repair at his car dealer, a customer has to deal with this insult. The auto mechanic carelessly slams the car hood down without first removing a large tool from the top of the engine, resulting in a dent in the hood. When the customer complains and asks that the dent be removed at the car dealer's expense, the mechanic says that the damage is so minor, it isn't worth fixing. Not worth fixing for whom? If you are subjected to this kind of customer service, ask to see the manager and say:

> *"My car was damaged in your garage while the engine was being repaired. I want the dent removed from my hood at no cost to me."*

If the manager minimizes the damage to your car, you can respond:

> *"Maybe you don't think that the damage is that bad, but I do and I want the dent removed from my car hood."*

If the manager pleads that his boss will throw a fit if he finds out about this, you can respond:

> *"I can't do anything about your problems with your boss. The hood of my car was damaged while the engine was being repaired in the garage you manage. I want the dent removed from the hood at no cost to me. If you can't handle this problem, please tell me whom to talk to about it."*

If the manager promises you a discount on a future repair, you can respond:

> *"I appreciate the offer for a discount on a future repair, but that is unnecessary. I want the dent removed from my car hood. Are you going to okay the repair or am I going to have to write a letter to the Better Business Bureau and the president of your company to get this matter resolved?"*

#37 "I DEMAND MY MONEY BACK!"

Everyone has eagerly purchased a product only to arrive home and discover that a crucial part is missing, the construction is flawed, or the item doesn't work right. It is annoying enough to have to take the time and return the product, but then to be frustrated by an employee who refuses to acknowledge and correct the problem is more than most people can bear.

Whether it is faulty electronic equipment, a pair of poorly sewn jeans, or a quart of sour milk, your strategy for returning the product remains the same. As a consumer you have the right to get what you pay for, and if you are dissatisfied, then you are entitled to a replacement or your money back. Remember to stay calm and polite, but firm. Use the "broken record" technique as many times as necessary until the other person complies. For example, if you bought a television that does not operate properly, tell the salesperson:

"I bought this television here yesterday and it is not operating properly. I'd like to exchange it for a new one, please."

If the salesperson suggests that their repair department can handle the problem, say:

"I'm sure your repair department is excellent, but that's not the point. I bought this television yesterday with the expectation that it would work properly. I'm not interested in getting this television repaired. I want a new one that works properly."

HOW TO ASK FOR A REFUND

Here are some ways to ask for a refund in spite of what the salesperson says to convince you otherwise.

You can say:

"I bought this television from your store, and it doesn't work properly, so I'd like a refund, please."

If the salesperson says:

"We can fix this television set, no problem. I'll have the part replaced and it will be good as new! You can pick it up tomorrow."

You can respond:

"I don't care if it can be fixed or not. I want a refund. May I speak to the store manager, please?"

If the salesperson says:

"The store manager is very busy right now. I can help you with this little problem."

You can respond:

"I'm sure the store manager is very busy, but so am I. Quite frankly, you're not being much help with this problem. What is the manager's name?"

You can tell the manager:

"I bought this television yesterday, and it doesn't work. I don't see any sign that says 'No refunds,' so I'd like my money back, please."

If the manager says:

"We can't return this set to the manufacturer. We can either repair the television set or exchange it. Say, I've got an idea! We've got a thirty-inch color floor model on sale, and I'll give you an additional ten percent discount! Now, there's a deal you can't refuse!"

You can respond:

"Your arrangement with the manufacturer is not my concern. I don't want another television set. I want a full refund. Are you going to refund my money, or am I going to have to talk to the company president and the Better Business Bureau?"

#38 "I EXPECT A PERFECT JOB!"

You thought you hired the best person to replace the broken tiles in your bathroom, but when the so-called expert finished, you were less than enthusiastic about the results. Next to poor customer service, inferior workmanship is a frequent consumer complaint. There is no reason to accept amateur results when you pay professional prices for work.

To keep the quality of a contractor's work up to par, first discuss what work is to be done, who is doing the work, and when it is to be finished. Be sure to set high standards from the beginning of the project, and periodically check the contractor's progress. Here are a few examples of how to set the tone and underscore what you expect in terms of workmanship. You can say:

"Before you begin the job, let's put down on paper exactly what you plan to do and when you expect to finish."

If the contractor says:

"That won't be necessary. I know what to do."

You can respond:

"I'm sure you do know what to do, but I just want to make sure we both agree on exactly what you are going to do, about how long it will take, how much it will cost, and what I expect from you. I don't want any loose ends or messes left for me to clean up. Also, if you come up against a problem that will change anything in our agreement, I want you to stop working and tell me right away."

Once the work is underway, look in every so often and say:

"How are things going? Any problems? Is the work going according to schedule?"

If you spot a problem that the worker seems to ignore, you can say:

"How are you going to handle this problem?"

If he plays down the problem, you can say:

> *"You may not think this is a big deal, but I do and I want it taken care of now. I don't want it left to the end of the job, because by then it will be too late to do anything about it. So how are you going to handle it?"*

Another method of keeping an eye on a contractor without making him feel that you are looking over his shoulder is to ask:

> *"Do you mind if I watch you for a while and learn how a real professional fixes a . . . ?"*

In most cases professional contractors don't mind if you watch them work as long as you don't get in their way or ask them too many questions.

#39 "I'M NOT PAYING FOR THIS JOB UNTIL IT'S DONE RIGHT!"

How many times have arrogant home-improvement contractors promised you a perfect job, only to leave you with a slew of unfinished minor details and a major mess when they ask for their check? To avoid this problem, have the contractor write down in a signed and dated contract: what work will be done; that only new material will be used; the date on which the work will begin and be completed; that he is responsible for cleaning up and removing waste; and that all workmanship and materials are fully guaranteed for a specific length of time.

Without a written agreement, you could be in for an argument about exactly what work was agreed upon. Since contractors are accustomed to this sort of after-the-fact negotiations, they often win concessions or more money from their naive clients. A written contract encourages contractors to complete the agreed-upon job before asking for the final payment. Here are several ways to counter a contractor's arguments that the job is finished when you feel it is not. You can say:

"Before I write the check, I want to make sure you've done everything that we agreed upon and that I am happy with it."

As you inspect the work, write down anything that does not comply with your agreement. Hand the list to the contractor and say:

"What you have done looks good, but there are still several final details and the cleanup that needs to be completed. I'll write your check when the job is finished."

If the contractor balks and says:

"Look, this job has taken longer than I thought, and I'm scheduled to start another job this afternoon. Can you pay me for the job now, and I'll take care of those details tomorrow?"

You can respond:

"I'm sure you want to get paid and that you need to get on to your next job. But according to our contract the job isn't finished. I think it is only fair to pay you when you finish the job."

#40 "YOUR ADVICE WAS DEAD WRONG!"

Has this ever happened to you? Your accountant tells you to expect a $1,000 income tax refund. However, instead of a check, you get a letter from the IRS saying your tax return has a mistake and you owe them an additional $1,500, plus a large penalty! After getting up off the floor, you call your accountant and start screaming at her over the telephone.

Everyone receives poor or incorrect professional advice from time to time. Before you threaten to sue your doctor, lawyer, or accountant, remember that even highly trained professionals make mistakes. The most effective strategy for dealing with a professional who goofs or whose opinion you do not agree with is to stay cool, be professional yourself, and offer an opportunity to correct the error. Here are several examples of what you can say to various professionals:

To your accountant:

> *"I know everyone expects you to be perfect, but there seems to be a serious mistake on my tax return. I'm not happy about it, but I'm sure you can correct it."*

To your doctor:

> *"I'm sure your advice is good, but I'm not happy with how my medication makes me feel. One kind of pill makes me drowsy and the other one makes me feel like I drank five cups of coffee. I want to reevaluate my medication so that I can stop taking so many pills."*

To your financial adviser:

> *"I understand that you can't predict the rise and fall of the market, but those stocks you told me to buy just dropped ten points! I'm not comfortable with that kind of risk. I want to change my portfolio to more conservative investments. Can you help me do that, or should I find another adviser?"*

#41 "PAY YOUR BILL, OR ELSE!"

Do you have clients or renters who owe you money or who are chronically late with their payments? Deadbeats can kill a small business or erase rental income, yet many people are reluctant to press others for overdue payments because they want to maintain goodwill. True, checks get lost in the mail and accounting departments make mistakes. Whatever the reason for not getting paid, the sooner you address late-payment problems, the more likely you'll be to get your money. The longer you wait, the harder it is to collect.

You can save yourself a lot of headaches and volatile conversations if you set the financial terms of any business agreement at the outset. For example if you are renting a house, be sure to repeat aloud what is included in the lease. You can say:

> *"I just want to make sure you understand what is written in the lease. The rent is due on . . . and there is a deposit of . . . dollars. Do you have any problems with that?"*

In other business situations you can send a delinquency notice if the payment is ten days late to remind a forgetful client to pay up. This way you can head off the tense discussions that usually accompany telephone calls for money owed. If your reminder fails, however, you will need to phone the person responsible. Keep your voice calm, spell out the problem briefly, but never make threats. Here are some examples of what you can say:

> *"I am calling to find out why I haven't received your check. What seems to be the problem?"*

If the person replies:

> *"I'm sorry, but we're behind in our payments because we've recently lost a few people in our department, and I'm the only one left."*

You can respond:

> *"I'm sure you are overworked and understaffed, but I need you to send me a check for . . . dollars. When can I expect it?"*

If the person tries to stall you by saying:

> *"We are having a bit of a cash-flow problem. We'll send you a check as soon as we can."*

You can respond:

> *"I understand that cash flow is a problem, but I have to pay my bills too. Your payment is overdue, and I cannot let it go any longer. When can I expect your check?"*

As a last resort you may have to talk to a company officer and present a "veiled threat," such as:

> *"You must pay me the money, and there's no negotiating that point. I will take further action if I have to, but I'd rather not. Why don't you just write me a check right now and that will be the end of this problem and save you a lot of time and trouble. How about it?"*

PERSISTENCE MOTIVATES OTHERS TO ACT

Your stick-to-itiveness demonstrates that you will not give up or get sidetracked from getting the customer service you want or the payment you deserve. It may take several assertive conversations to get satisfaction, but if you persevere, you will usually get your way. It is wise to keep a written record of the date, names of people you talked to, and a brief description of each conversation. If it becomes necessary to contact the Better Business Bureau, company president, local newspaper, consumer complaint bureau, or small claims court, then you'll have specific facts to back up your side of the story.

DOS AND DON'TS FOR CONVERSATIONS
IN COMMERCIAL SITUATIONS

Do remain polite and respectful.

Don't lose your temper, become hostile, or make specific threats.

Do talk to the person who can resolve your problem.

Don't repeat the problem to people who cannot resolve the issue.

Do know and exercise your consumer rights.

Don't let a business person put his or her needs before yours.

Do say how you want the issue resolved, as many times as necessary.

Don't get distracted by irrelevant questions, explanations, or excuses.

Do keep detailed records of your business conversations.

Don't be bullied into dropping your complaint, accepting poor customer service, or receiving less money than you deserve.

PART III

TACTFUL TALK IN YOUR PERSONAL RELATIONSHIPS

CHAPTER 10

Tactful Ways to Tell Your Friends . . .

"Do not use a hatchet to remove a fly from your friend's forehead."
—CHINESE PROVERB

The most enduring friendships are built on trust and take time to develop. However, tactlessly blurting out your opinions— even if they are with the best of intentions—can quickly ruin even the best of friendships. You need to maintain a delicate balance between speaking openly, offering gentle suggestions, and quietly accepting a friend's decisions. Here are some common situations that can cause problems between friends, and how to handle them tactfully.

#42 "DON'T HOG THE CONVERSATION!"

Some people just love to hear the sound of their own voice. If your friend tends to blab on nonstop, first try a light approach to tell him that he is talking excessively. You could say:

"How many cups of coffee did you have this morning? You're talking a blue streak!"

"You've been jabbering for ten minutes straight! Take a break. Besides, I want to tell you something that I'm very excited about."

If your friend persists in bombarding you with another long-winded example, be more direct. Begin with your friend's name, and in a calm voice say one or more of the following statements:

"Alice, I can't seem to get a word in edgewise! I'd like to say something. Do you mind letting me have a turn to talk?"

"Tony, I understand that you are upset because . . . , but give me a chance to say something, please!"

"Grace, can you stop talking for a moment? I feel a little frustrated because you go on and on and don't seem to want to hear what I have to say. Can I say something now?"

HOW TO STOP A CHATTERBOX

People talk incessantly because they are nervous, uncomfortable with silence, or want to impress you with the breadth of their knowledge. Here is a three-step method for stopping a friend who talks too much.

Step 1: Interrupt with two or three closed-ended questions that require only a one- or two-word answer. This breaks the talkative person's flow of words and shows that you are listening and that you want to talk. For example:

"What time did you get to the party?"

"Who was there?"

"Did you meet anyone interesting?"

Step 2: After your friend answers the questions, start talking immediately and share a related experience. If you don't start talking right away, the chatterbox will pick up right where he or she left off. Don't ask another question or stop talking until you are ready to give up the conversational ball! You can say:

"Speaking of meeting people, I met an interesting guy while I was walking my dog in the park. His dog ran right over to

mine, so we started talking and found out that we both are taking classes at. . . ."

Step 3: Don't allow the chatterbox to interrupt you. You can say:

"Wait, please don't interrupt me. I'm not finished talking yet."

#43 "I DAMAGED SOMETHING OF YOURS."

What do you say when you break a tool, camera, or other possession loaned to you by a friend? Your first inclination may be to deny your guilt, downplay the extent of the damage, or minimize the value of the item. These reactions, however, will probably just make your friend angry.

The tactful way to tell about damaging a borrowed item is simply to explain what happened without overdramatizing or minimizing the incident. Then accept responsibility, apologize, and offer to do whatever is necessary to correct the problem. Here are three examples of how to accept responsibility for damaging someone's property:

"Jay, I have some bad news to tell you about your car. I smashed the right taillight, but I'll pay to get it fixed. I'll take it to the auto body shop today and have it repaired. They'll loan you a car while it's getting fixed. I'm so sorry that it happened."

"Maria, I can't return your leather jacket today because I tore the sleeve on a nail, so I took it to a tailor to be mended. I feel terrible because I know this is your favorite jacket, but the tailor guaranteed me that you'll never see the repair. I hope you're not too upset. I'm awfully sorry."

"Dad, I had a problem with the power saw you loaned me. For some reason the motor just stopped running. I know you need a saw for work, so I bought you a new one and I'll see if I can get this one fixed."

#44 "I DON'T WANT TO HEAR ALL YOUR PROBLEMS."

Do you have a friend who loves to talk about his or her troubled personal life? Frustrating though it may be, part of being a good friend is being a sympathetic listener. There comes a point, however, when even your best friend can bore you to tears and drive you away by going on about problems in his or her love life, job, or family.

How can you tell your friend that you have heard enough without sounding insensitive or uncaring? First, show your compassion by acknowledging your friend's feelings. Then be supportive by saying that you have confidence in his or her ability to find a solution. Add that you don't have any answers and then swiftly change to a more interesting and positive subject. Here are some ways tactfully to change the subject:

> *"I can see that your job is really troubling you. I wish I knew what to tell you, but I don't know the answer. I'm sure you'll figure something out. To change the subject, I've been meaning to ask you about. . . ."*

> *"I'm sorry to hear that your love life is so messed up. I really don't know what to say except that if you're not happy, make some changes. And speaking of change, I've been meaning to tell you about my plans to. . . ."*

If your friend persists in dwelling upon his or her problems, then you may have to be more direct and say in an understanding, yet assertive tone:

> *"I feel badly for you, but we seem to keep having this same conversation over and over. Would you mind if we talked about something else?"*

#45 "YOU NEED PROFESSIONAL HELP."

Do you have a friend who has extreme difficulty coping with his or her personal problems? Does your friend constantly call you in tears asking for advice and support, yet remains paralyzed, overwhelmed, making the same mistakes over and over? When does a person need professional help? Most mental health professionals agree that everyone makes mistakes, but people need professional help when they continually repeat their mistakes.

How can you suggest that your friend seek the services of a mental health professional without sounding condescending or critical? Your friend may be more receptive if you phrase your suggestion in the form of a question, especially when he or she is asking you for advice. Avoid criticizing past mistakes or offering specific solutions. First rephrase your friend's situation to show you were listening and then follow with a gentle question. Here are three examples:

> *"It sounds as if you feel very frustrated and overwhelmed with all your problems. Have you ever considered getting some professional advice to help you find some solutions?"*

> *"You are obviously frustrated with. . . . Why not get a referral and talk to a therapist, who can give you some professional help? It might make a big difference. Besides, what have you got to lose?"*

> *"If you're so upset and don't know what to do, why don't you get some professional help?"*

If your friend hesitates and says:

> *"Oh, I don't know. The thought of talking to a therapist makes me nervous. You never know what a shrink might ask or find out! Plus, I don't want some stranger telling me what to do."*

You can respond:

> *"I agree with you that it's scary to make decisions, but a good therapist will give you feedback and help you come to your own conclusions. I know a therapist you might like. Why not give her a call and see what she has to say?"*

#46 "WE WEREN'T MEANT TO BE ROOMMATES."

Did your best friend ask you to share an apartment and you agreed because it seemed like a good idea at the time? Now, however, you've found that because your lifestyles are too dif-

ferent, you've changed your mind. How do you tell your roommate that for the sake of the friendship you have decided to
move out? Here is how you can bring up the topic:
    You can say:

*"Bob, I've got to talk to you. Could you turn the stereo
down so that we can hear each other?"*

If your friend says:

*"What? Too loud for you? Hey, isn't this a great tune? I've
invited some of the gang over. It's party time!"*

You can say:

*"Look, Bob, that's what I want to talk to you about. I've
decided that I'm going to look for another place to live. It's
nothing personal, after all you're my best friend. It's just
that I can't study with all the loud music and the people
over here all the time."*

If your friend says:

*"Oh, come on, you're just mad because I always leave my
dishes in the sink!"*

You can say:

*"Well, I don't like cleaning up after you, that's for sure.
But, our lifestyles are just too different. You like to order
food in for dinner, and I can't afford to do that. You like to
party all night, and I have to study and attend early classes.
I'm afraid that if we stay roommates, it's going to mess up
our friendship, and I don't want that to happen. I've made
plans to move at the end of next month to give you time to
find another roommate. But you're still my best friend."*

#47 "I SPILLED THE BEANS!"

As friends confide in each other, their mutual trust and friendship grow. Breaching this pact by revealing private information
to others will severely damage the relationship if your friend

finds out. But what happens if you accidentally slip and reveal your friend's secret? Should you pretend that your indiscretion did not happen or should you confess your blunder? If your friend finds out from a third party that you were the one who let the cat out of the bag, then be prepared for a quick end to your friendship.

On the other hand, if you explain that your gaffe was an honest mistake or a lapse in judgment, your friend may forgive you. No matter how your friend reacts, be prepared for angry words and a cooling off of your friendship. This is tough, but you can say something like:

> *"I did something really stupid that is going to make you mad. I accidentally told . . . that you are. . . ."*

If your friend blows up and says:

> *"I can't believe you and your big mouth! Especially after you promised to keep it a secret!"*

You can respond:

> *"I don't blame you for being mad. I know you said not to tell anyone, and I blew it. I wanted to be the one to tell you so that you wouldn't think I was talking behind your back. If you never want to speak to me again, I'll understand, but I'm really sorry and I feel terrible. I hope you can forgive me, because I still want to be your friend."*

#48 "I'M ANGRY! YOU HURT MY FEELINGS!"

Do you remember the last time a friend said something that hurt your feelings or made you mad? Maybe he or she said something hurtful or revealed a secret of yours. When this happens, the only thing you can do is say something. After all, your friend can't read your mind, so it is up to you to tell your friend how he or she has offended you. Keep the following points in mind when you bring up the subject.

Your friend may:

- Be completely unaware that your feelings have been hurt.
- Assume that his or her behavior does not offend you.
- Assume that because you are friends, you will excuse insensitive or inappropriate behavior.

Your friend may be a little embarrassed or defensive to hear that he or she did something to upset you. However, if you speak calmly, directly, and use a confident tone of voice, your friendship will probably grow even stronger. All you have to do is say something like:

> *"I want you to know that it really hurts my feelings when you. . . ."*

If your friend claims:

> *"Wait a second! What are you getting so upset about? I didn't do anything! Anyway, I was just kidding when I said. . . ."*

You can say:

> *"You may not realize it, but when you constantly tease me about . . . in front of people I don't know, it makes me feel uncomfortable and a little angry. I begin to wonder if you really mean what you're saying. Do you?"*

If your friend says:

> *"Of course I don't mean it. I'm just having a little fun, that's all. Really. I didn't know that it was upsetting you."*

You can respond:

> *"I didn't think that you did, that's why I'm asking you to stop. I don't want to make a big deal about it, but I don't really appreciate being the butt of your jokes, okay?"*

#49 "I'M GLAD YOU GOT A DIVORCE!"

What do you say to a friend who after years of being stuck in an unhappy relationship finally gets divorced? Do you jump for joy, berate his or her ex-spouse, or satisfy your own curiosity by asking personal questions?

Since your friend is probably feeling a wide range of emotions, from extreme relief to severe depression, keep your opinions to yourself, be a good listener, and let him or her do most of the talking. In this situation it's what you don't say that will save you from making tactless comments and embarrassing your friend.

Here are several things *not* to say:

"Everyone thought you were the perfect couple. What happened?"

"I knew your marriage would never last. Why did you marry that jerk in the first place?"

"I'm surprised your marriage lasted as long as it did."

"I was wondering how long it was going to take for you to come to your senses."

"Who asked for the divorce?"

"Was there someone else?"

"What did your family say?"

What is the best thing to say to your newly divorced friend? Since congratulations or pity are inappropriate, you can simply say:

"I'm sorry to hear things didn't work out."

"Getting a divorce is a tough situation, but you'll be okay. You're a survivor."

"How are you feeling?"

#50 "I'M DATING YOUR FORMER BOYFRIEND (GIRLFRIEND)."

What would be more threatening to a friendship than dating your friend's ex-spouse or lover? Before you jump into this sticky situation, consider these points:

- Was the breakup mutual or was one party jilted?
- Has sufficient time passed for both people to get on with their separate lives?
- Is your friend involved in a new relationship?
- How does your friend feel about his or her past relationship?
- Is your friend angry or bitter about the past relationship?
- Does your friend hope to get back together with his or her ex?
- Does the past lover have an ulterior motive for dating you?
- What do you think your friend's gut reaction will be to your dating his or her ex?
- Are you willing to risk your friendship to become romantically involved with this person?

Jumping into a relationship with a friend's ex-lover could easily damage your friendship beyond repair. If you have not yet begun dating the ex, you could bring the subject up and see how your friend reacts to the idea. Listen carefully and watch your friend's response. He or she might say, *"No problem, why should I care?"* but really feel uncomfortable with the idea. Here are two examples of what you can say:

> *"Lee, I've been wondering how you might feel if I asked Jenny out for a date. I know you broke up last month, but if it would make you feel uncomfortable, I won't ask her. Our friendship means a lot to me, and I wouldn't want to mess it up."*

> *"Jody, your ex-boyfriend asked me out on a date. Since you two broke up and you're dating other people, I was wondering if you had any objections to me going out with him. He seems like a nice guy, but if it would upset you, I'll say no."*

If you have already been dating and want to tell your friend that you are now romantically involved with his or her ex, then you can say:

> *"Nancy, there is something that I want to tell you before you find out from someone else. Harry and I have been dating for about a month and we really like each other. You're my best friend, and I wouldn't want to do anything to hurt you, but I wasn't sure how you would react when you found out. I figured that since your divorce from Harry became final last year, it would be okay for us to date. Am I right?"*

#51 "I'D LIKE A DATE WITH YOU."

Do you find it difficult to ask a friend or acquaintance for a date? To help overcome your fear of rejection, first extend an informal invitation to spend time together and see how the other person responds. You can say something like:

> *"Jan, I really enjoyed meeting you at your sister's wedding. What do you say we go dancing sometime?"*

> *"Jack, I like playing tennis with you. Are you interested in joining me for a little cool refreshment?"*

> *"Susan, if you're not busy after work, would you like to join me for dinner and a movie?"*

If the other person responds positively to your initial overture, the chances are good that he or she will accept an invitation for a specific date. Generally the more specific the activity you suggest, the more likely you'll be to elicit an enthusiastic acceptance, or else a polite refusal with the possibility of a date at a more convenient time. Here are several more examples of how to ask for a date:

> *"I have an extra seat at the ball game (theater, concert, etc.) for Thursday evening. I'd be really happy if you joined me. We could get a bite to eat afterward! It will be lots of fun."*

"Since you said you love ethnic food, I'd love to take you out to a great Italian restaurant I know next Friday night— that is, if you're not busy."

"My hiking club is going on a half-day hike next Sunday. The people are really friendly, and guests are always welcome. I sure would like it if you would join me."

HOW TO GIVE A SOFT REJECTION

Refusing an offer for a date usually falls into one of two categories: a polite refusal without further encouragement and a qualified *no* with the possibility of *yes* at a later date.

Here are some examples of soft rejections that tell the other person that you may be available to go out at some other time:

"Sorry, I'm busy this Friday night, but I'd love to go out with you next weekend."

"I'm usually too tired for a movie after work, but maybe we can go out for a cup of coffee or a quick bite to eat."

"I'd love to go to the game with you, but I've already made plans for Saturday. But I would love to go, so maybe we could go some other time."

If you don't want to go out on a date with someone, don't make up elaborate excuses. Simply say in a friendly, but firm manner:

"I'm not really interested, but thanks for asking."

Always accept a rejection gracefully. Consider three rejections as a good indication that the other person does not want to go out with you, and don't ask again. Also remember that being rejected for a date is not the end of the world. Just look for someone else who is more receptive to spending time with you.

You can say:

"No problem. I just thought I'd ask."

#52 "I WANT TO BE MORE THAN JUST FRIENDS."

Perhaps the most delicate situation in a friendship is when one friend wants to change a platonic relationship into something more romantic. What can you say to let your feelings be known without making a fool of yourself or embarrassing your friend? How do you know if your friend feels the same as you? Is it even a good idea to fall in love with a friend? What are the risks?

There are risks in attempting to change a friendship into a romance. If your gamble succeeds, you will have the best of both worlds—a friend who is your lover too. On the other hand, if romance with your friend is not in the cards, your friendship can survive and continue to grow, although it may slow down and take some time to recover.

Before you take the leap into love with a friend, honestly ask yourself if the two of you share enough common interests, values, and goals to make a love relationship work. If the answer is no, then you are probably better off leaving your relationship as is. If, however, you feel there might be a potential for a romance, then just speak your heart and say something like:

> *"I've been dating other people for over a year now, and you know something, I'd rather be with you than anyone else. I guess I'm saying I like you more than just a friend."*

> *"I know this may sound funny, us being friends and all, but I feel closer to you than anyone else I know. I really like you a lot—and I mean more than just a friend."*

> *"I'm not sure how to say this, but my feelings for you have changed over the last few months. I want to be more than just friends."*

HOW TO HANDLE A REJECTION

While your emotions may be close to the surface, your amorous advances might catch your friend by surprise and as a result elicit a negative response. If this happens, don't pressure your friend into saying or doing anything that he or she is not ready

for. In other words, if your friend rejects your romantic over-
tures, then accept the rejection gracefully by saying:

> *"I didn't mean to embarrass you or put you on the spot. I
> just wanted to tell you how I'm feeling because I was hop-
> ing you might be feeling the same way. I understand that
> you don't feel as I do and I accept that, but let me know if
> you ever change your mind!"*

Tips for First Dates

- Show your sense of humor and that you like to have fun.
- Plan a casual activity that allows you and your date to get to
  know each other.
- Find out what the other person likes to do for fun.
- Be open to trying new activities.
- Talk about light and upbeat subjects.
- Don't be too anxious to get physical.
- If you are having a good time, take your date's arm in yours.
- At the end of the evening say you enjoyed the time you
  spent together, give your date a warm smile and lingering
  look, then a hug and kiss good night.
- If you're not interested in dating him or her again, a smile,
  handshake, and polite thank-you will do.
- If you want to go out again, call soon for a follow-up date.

CHAPTER 11

Tactful Ways to Tell Your Date, Sweetheart, or Fiancé . . .

For most teens and young adults the dating game is an exciting ritual for finding a mate. However, for many divorced, widowed, or adult singles, dating is an uncomfortable and dreary experience. They forget that lengthy monologues about deceased spouses, failed relationships, or misplaced career priorities are not particularly enticing or interesting to a prospective mate—at least not in the early stages of courtship.

Whether you are an eager rookie just beginning to date or a returning veteran, here are some of the hardest things to say to a potential companion, and tactful ways to say them.

#53 "I WANT TO KNOW IF YOU ARE AVAILABLE FOR A RELATIONSHIP."

Don't assume that just because you are single, the person you are dating is also unattached. Lack of a wedding band does not necessarily mean a person is single either. If you date someone a few times, it's wise to find out whether he or she is available for a relationship or is seriously involved with someone else.

While it may feel awkward to bring up the subject of availability, it is best to get this vital information out in the open as soon as possible. The most desirable answer is that both of you are unattached and available to see each other on a regular basis—if that is what both of you elect to do. Here are some tactful ways to ask if the other person is free to pursue a more intimate relationship. You can take a plain approach and say:

"Excuse me for being so direct, but are you married or living with someone?"

"Do you have a steady boyfriend (girlfriend)?"

"Do you date a lot?"

"Are you seeing someone on a steady basis?"

"Do you have anyone special in your life?"

Here are some ways to let the other person know that you are unattached and available:

"I date a few people here and there, but there's no one special in my life right now. What about you? Do you have anyone special?"

"Now that I've finished school, I'm getting back into the dating scene. I've gone out with some different people, but you're the first person that I've met that I really enjoy spending time with."

"After being divorced for two years I feel like I'm ready to start having fun with other people again."

"I really like going out with you. I hope we can keep seeing each other."

#54 "I'M BREAKING OUR DATE."

Breaking dates is annoying at best, downright rude if it happens more than twice, and can be an indirect signal that the other person has little interest in continuing the dating relationship. Making feeble or tactless excuses does little to relieve the aggravation and often causes permanent damage to a budding relationship. However, it is sometimes necessary to cancel a social engagement. Here are some basic rules you can follow:

- Call as far ahead of time as possible to cancel.
- Avoid making up a "big lie," such as suddenly being called out of town or needing to take a sick friend to the hospital.
- Say that circumstances beyond your control are the reason for breaking the date. For example, your boss demanded that you work late, a water pipe broke and you need to wait for a plumber, or your brother-in-law forgot to tell you about a family birthday dinner.
- Never suggest that a more interesting offer came along.
- Always offer a sincere apology and admit that you have inconvenienced the other person.
- Quickly suggest a new day and time to meet in the near future.

Here is an example of a tact*less* excuse left on the answering machine:

"Betty, a new client just invited me to join him for dinner tonight, so I'm going to have to skip out on our date tonight. Since you and I can go out any time, I'll call you later and we can set something up."

Here is an example of a tact*ful* excuse:

"Frank, I'm sorry, but I'm not going to be able to make our dinner date for Thursday. My boss just ordered me to attend an evening emergency client meeting, and I'm sure it is going to run late. I apologize for canceling, but I called you as soon as I found out. Can we meet for dinner Friday night instead? If you're busy, I'll understand, but I hope we can see each other soon."

#55 "LET'S HAVE SEX!"

How do you communicate your desire to have intimate relations with someone you are dating? Does flirting send a clear message that you feel amorous toward your date? Is it better to make a sexually inviting gesture (also known as a pass), or should you try to seduce him or her? Giving your friend a passionate kiss, for example, can indicate that you are eager to become sexually intimate. If your physical gesture is genuine and enticing and your partner is receptive to the idea, then it can come as a welcome invitation. In this situation your warm smiles, intimate eye contact, hugs, kisses, and gentle touching speak far more loudly than words, but you may want to add something like:

"I've been wanting to get close to you for a long time."

"Are you feeling the same way about me right now as I'm feeling about you?"

"Nothing would make me happier than to make love with you. How do you feel about that?"

If you get a positive response, then just let nature take its course, and don't forget to use protection! If, on the other hand, your pass is rough, crude, or ill timed, then your potential lover may consider your request vulgar and unromantic. Most romantic individuals like flirting and seduction because they create anticipation and heighten the excitement and romance of sex. Flirting sends a message of sexual interest through innuendo and body language. Seduction can follow by suggesting an activity that will likely lead to lovemaking. For example:

"Would you like to come to my place tonight for a little dinner? I'm a great cook, and I'd really like to whip up something special just for you!"

"I know a quiet place where we can be alone."

"How about us going away together for the weekend?"

#56 "GET YOUR HANDS OFF ME!"

In the beginning most dates consist of a lot of entertainment, some eating, and a hint of affection. As two people continue to date, the amount of affection usually increases. While it is natural for two people to test each other's sexual limits, confusion arises if one person is more aggressive than the other. If this happens, it is vital that the unwilling person speak up and let the anxious romantic know that his or her sexual advances are premature or unwelcome.

Say no to unwanted romantic attention by sending a firm and consistent message that you are uncomfortable with the sexual advances and that you want them to stop. Look the person straight in the eyes, keep your head and chin upright, and speak in a calm, strong voice. Here are several examples of how to say no to your date's sexual advances:

"Hey, stop touching me like that! I don't like what you are doing and I want you to stop."

"Stop what you are doing right now!"

"I don't want to do anything more than kiss you!"

If your date replies:

"Oh, come on, what are you afraid of? I'm not going to hurt you. You'll like it. I've got plenty of experience in this department and know just what to do. Trust me. Okay?"

You can respond firmly:

"No, I don't trust you! You are obviously not getting the message that I don't like what you're doing and that I want you to stop. You're making me feel uncomfortable. I think it's time for you to take me home. Do you understand?"

#57 "I HOPE YOU'RE HEALTHY."

Are you dating someone with whom you may want to become sexually involved, but you are afraid to get intimate because he or she might have a sexually transmitted disease? Before you find yourself caught up in a passionate embrace that can lead to a sexual encounter, find out if the other person is concerned or nonchalant about sex and sexually transmitted diseases. You may feel a little uncomfortable discussing this topic, but talking about it is one way to avoid making a sexual mistake that can affect your health. Share your own opinions and attitudes about casual sexual relationships and find out how your prospective partner feels too. The greater a person's awareness of how to avoid sexually transmitted diseases and how to prevent them, the more likely it is that he or she uses some form of protection.

A casual way to bring up the subject of casual sex and sexually transmitted diseases is to discuss what you read, hear, and see in the media. Here are some ways to steer the conversation toward this sensitive subject, explain your views, and openly discuss protection before you get sexually involved:

> *"Did you happen to see the movie . . . ? I thought it was great that the main characters used condoms during the love scenes. I think it's good that movies show safe sex. What do you think about that?"*

> *"Can you believe the sex they show on daytime television? I like sex, but I'd be afraid to be that promiscuous with all the scary diseases that are floating around these days. How do you avoid catching sexually transmitted diseases?"*

> *"I just read another article on AIDS and heterosexuals. I think it is really scary because you never know if someone you might have sex with is HIV positive or has some other sexually transmitted disease. How do you handle this situation?"*

> *"This may sound rather direct, but what do you use for protection against diseases and to avoid pregnancy?"*

> *"I know this can be a little embarrassing to talk about, but I think it's important that we talk about protection before we get too physically involved."*

#58 "I HAVE A DARK SECRET."

Revealing to a new friend that you have an ongoing health problem, sexually transmitted disease, or criminal record is an embarrassing and agonizing experience. Even though disclosing personal information builds rapport and trust between two people and allows the relationship to grow, you may feel uncomfortable about discussing some aspects of your life. What is the best way to disclose a deep, dark secret from your past? When is the best time to tell a potential lover such personal information or to disclose a past indiscretion? What kind of personal information is better left unsaid? How will your new friend react? Will he or she be shocked and angry and perhaps withdraw from you, never to be seen or heard from again? Or will your new companion be understanding and willing to work around the problem?

One way to help answer these questions is to ask yourself if keeping a particular secret puts your partner at risk or affects the well-being and future of your present relationship. It is also important to put the revelation in perspective. Is it life-threatening, merely inconvenient, or simply past history?

For example, have you:

- Contracted a sexually transmitted disease?
- Been physically or emotionally abused in a previous marriage?
- Abused drugs or alcohol?
- Been diagnosed with a mental or physical illness?
- Gone bankrupt?
- Been arrested for tax evasion?
- Served time in prison?

While secrets like these may be difficult to reveal, they are best to get out in the open early in your relationship. If you do have a contagious medical condition, it is vital that you reveal its nature *before* it becomes the other person's problem or before you find yourself in the heat of a passionate embrace. Besides, if you continue to date the person, he or she is going to find out about the problem sooner or later. As far as timing is concerned, bring up sensitive subjects in private when both of you are calm and have time to discuss them in some detail.

You can say:

"I have to tell you something that is very difficult and embarrassing for me to say. I have a mild case of herpes that comes and goes. It's not life-threatening, just damn incon-

venient. I want to keep seeing you, but I'll understand if you want to stop going out with me."

While there is no way of telling how your friend will respond to difficult revelations, dealing honestly and directly with the issue will increase your chances of maintaining a new relationship. Here are several more examples of how to make an embarrassing revelation.

You can open the conversation by saying:

"Now that we are getting to know each other better, there is something that I've kept to myself, but that I want you to know. . . .

"I'm seeing a therapist because I was terribly abused in my first marriage and I'm still learning how to deal with my anger."

"I am a recovering alcoholic and drug addict. I've been sober for five years."

"I once filed for bankruptcy, but my accountant says that my credit is absolutely perfect and that my business is in excellent shape."

"I was diagnosed with skin cancer five years ago. I've had treatment and it is in remission, but I feel you have a right to know."

"I used to take drugs and drink a lot."

"I was thrown out of high school when I was fourteen, but I went back and earned my Graduate Equivalent Diploma."

"I served some time in jail."

"I've been married and divorced three times."

"I was abused as a child."

Most people are afraid to disclose these kinds of secrets because they fear being looked down upon and losing the other person—and sometimes that is exactly what happens. Revealing a dark secret can be risky, but it can also tell you as much about your friend as it tells your friend about you. Was he or she judgmental or understanding? Did telling your secret create a stronger bond and sense of mutual trust between you, or did your friend clam up and withdraw from your relationship?

To find out how your new friend feels about your revelation, ask:

"Now that I've told you my little secret, do you want to talk about it? How do you feel about what I've told you?"

WORDS OF CAUTION ABOUT REVEALING SECRETS

- Some secrets are better left unrevealed. Don't let anyone pressure you into disclosing a secret. Decide what is best for you and your relationship.
- When in doubt, keep a secret to yourself until you know your partner better.
- You don't have to tell your new lover everything about your checkered past—at least not right away.
- Revealing a secret may cost you your new love relationship. But if the person cannot accept you and your not-so-perfect past, you may be better off without him or her.
- Never cast your new friend in the role of someone to whom you confess your past sins, especially if there is nothing either of you can do about them now.
- If you feel guilty about or are preoccupied by some past event, decision, or indiscreet behavior, then discuss the situation in private with your priest, rabbi, pastor, or mental health professional before you disclose the secret to your new partner.

#59 "I'M NOT READY TO HAVE SEX WITH YOU."

It is amazing how many men still assume that the money they spend on a woman for dinner and entertainment can be redeemed at the end of the evening in the form of sex. The sooner men eliminate this commercial approach to sex and dating, the better it will be for both sexes. An acceptable response to such a tactless request can be:

> *"I'm absolutely astounded that you think I owe you sex in return for you buying me dinner! What do you think I am, a hooker? Here's my share of the bill, so now we're even. Good night and good-bye!"*

If you are not interested in or ready for sex, you are under no obligation to become intimate with anyone—no matter what he or she has done for you. A cool but direct and somewhat gracious approach is best in this situation. Here are several examples of ways to say no to sex. Be prepared to use the "broken record" technique, especially if you are being pursued by a persistent romantic who is "hot to trot."
You can say:

> *"I don't want to become sexually involved with you."*

If the other person says:

> *"You're so beautiful (handsome). I really want to get close to you. Come on, let's get it on!"*

You can respond:

> *"I find you very attractive, too, but I'm not ready to have sex with you. I need to know you better."*

If the Romeo says:

> *"I'm a fantastic lover."*

You can refuse the offer by responding:

> *"I'm sure you are, but I'm not ready to get that physically involved."*

If your admirer says:

"I want you so bad."

You can respond:

"I'm flattered that you find me so desirable, but I've decided that it's not a good idea to have sex with you."

If your suitor tries to manipulate you by saying:

"If you really love me as much as you say, you'd have sex with me."

You can stand up to the pressure by responding:

"I do love you, but I have to do what I think is best for me."

If you get this desperate plea:

"I just want us to have a little fun together. Come on, just this once and I'll never ask you again. What do you say?"

You can end the discussion by responding:

"That doesn't sound like the kind of relationship I'm looking for. Forget about it, I'm not having sex with you!"

If you are not ready for a sexual encounter, but don't want to alienate the other person because you might want to have sex with him or her in the future, you can say:

"Look, I really like you, but I'm not ready to have sex with you. Let's get to know each other better before we get sexually involved."

#60 "YOU'RE NOT MY TYPE."

Dating and courtship is the time to find out all you can about a person before investing a lot of time and emotional energy in the relationship. In addition to compatible backgrounds, common interests, basic attitudes, similar values, and shared opinions, you want to determine if there is a true potential for a lasting relationship. To help you decide whether to continue dating a particular person, ask yourself the following questions:

- Does he or she make me feel good about myself?
- Do we treat each other with mutual respect?
- Do I enjoy the time we spend together?
- Is he or she available to spend time with me?
- Does he or she show curiosity and interest in me?
- Does our conversation flow easily from topic to topic?
- Have we discovered some common interests?
- Do we share some common opinions and attitudes?
- Do I feel comfortable revealing my feelings and opinions?
- Does he or she excite me physically?
- Have we discussed our attitudes about sex and drugs?
- Could this person become my good friend?
- Can I imagine myself and this person in a permanent love relationship?

If you answered yes to most of these questions, then continue your dating relationship, because it seems to have the potential for true romance. If you answered no to more than half of these questions and if your instincts tell you that this person may not be right for you, then seriously consider ending the dating relationship before you get too involved.

You can send the other person a signal that you are no longer interested in dating by suddenly being "too busy" to get together. While it may seem harsh, being unavailable is an indirect way of saying that you do not wish to continue the dating relationship—without having to painfully explain why this person does not measure up to your expectations. However, your suitor may insist on knowing the reasons for your sudden loss of interest, or you may prefer to be more direct. In either case avoid making excuses and giving detailed explanations such as, ***"After a lot of soul-searching, I decided to go back to my wife."*** Start with the person's name and say something like:

> *"Bill, after our fight last night I don't see much of a future for this relationship. We're just too different, so let's not go out anymore, okay? I hope you understand."*

If the jilted suitor responds:

"Gosh, I thought things between us were going great. What happened? I mean, everyone argues. What's the big deal? We've only been out on two dates!"

You can respond:

"Look, you're a terrific person, and I'm sure you're going to make someone a wonderful partner, but I'm not that person. Let's just leave it at that, okay? I'm sorry if you are upset, but that's how I feel about it."

#61 "I'M BREAKING UP WITH YOU."

Lori and Stan have been seeing each other exclusively for about a year and have even discussed the possibility of living together or getting married. Although their relationship began passionately, over the last several months it has degenerated into petty arguments followed by long periods of silent hostility.

They've talked about their communication problem but can't seem to get their relationship back on track. Lori wants to break up even though she likes Stan, because she now believes they have little in common and no future together. Stan loves having sex with Lori.

While he is not thrilled with their relationship, he figures "the devil you know is better than the devil you don't know." The question is, should Stan and Lori continue their relationship in this way or should they break up to find more suitable partners?

Breaking up is hard to do, but what could be worse than spending your life with the wrong person? While it is difficult to end a relationship, you can still do it tactfully. When you break up, avoid patronizing lines such as *"You're nice, but. . . ."* because they do not make the other person feel any better. It is preferable to offer some brief explanation of your decision to terminate the love relationship. Then claim equal responsibility for the affair not working out.

You can say with a calm but firm voice:

"This isn't easy for me to say, but this relationship has not been working for a long time. Our goals and values are just too different."

"We just don't seem to have fun together anymore. All we do is argue. We're really not right for each other. We've given this relationship a try and it didn't work. I think it's time we each go our own way."

"We want different things out of a relationship. I'm sure you could be much happier with someone else. I think it would be best if we both started seeing other people."

If your jilted lover then asks:

"Is it possible for us to still be friends?"

You can respond:

"Sure, why not? Just as long as you understand that it's a nonphysical relationship."

Note: Some people do remain friends after ending a more intimate relationship, but in most cases, when it's over—it's over.

#62 "WE OUGHT TO GET MARRIED."

Have you been dating someone special long enough to hear *"I want to marry this person"* repeating inside your head? Your inner voice is a good indication that you are ready to make a commitment to a permanent relationship, and all that stands in your way is—gulp!—popping the question, and of course a positive response. However, it is amazing how unromantic and tactless some partners can be at the most important crossroads of their relationship—proposing marriage. In this delicate situation it's not what you say that counts as much as what you *don't* say.

CAUTION: <u>DO NOT</u> PROPOSE MARRIAGE BY SAYING THE FOLLOWING:

"Why can't you make a commitment? If you really loved me, you'd marry me."

"Let's make a go of it and see what happens."

"Marry me, or I'll find someone else."

"My mother said she is tired of lying to her friends about us living together, so let's get married."

"My accountant says I could use the tax deduction and save over two thousand dollars if we get married before December thirty-first. What do you say?"

"Let's make our relationship official. A marriage certificate is only a piece of paper and won't change how I feel about you."

HOW TO PROPOSE MARRIAGE

If you want to marry your partner, then set the stage and present your proposal with gusto, confidence, and romance. If you are so inclined, you might want to go off together for a secluded romantic weekend and then pop the question near the end of your stay. Short of that, asking your partner to sit on a sofa beside you after a romantic evening will do. Then simply say something like:

"I can't live without you. Will you marry me?"

"I love you and want to live with you the rest of my life. Will you marry me?"

This method of proposing marriage is short, to the point, and yes, old-fashioned, but it has worked millions of times before and it can work for you too. Of course there is no guarantee that the other person shares your matrimonial desires, but at least you'll know that you gave the proposal your best shot!

#63 "THE MARRIAGE IS OFF!"

All your friends are saying, ***"You're engaged? Congratulations! You must be very happy!"*** But wait—now you're not so sure that getting married to this person is the right thing to do. There is an old saying with a new twist that goes something like, "Haste in marriage, repent in Reno." In other words, the faster you get into a marriage, the greater the chances it will end in divorce.

An engagement to be married is a trial period that tests a couple's patience, compatibility, and ability to compromise. If either person fails to live up to his or her partner's expectations during the engagement, then canceling the wedding may be the correct course of action. Granted, breaking an engagement will cause hard feelings, but that is much preferable to living together unhappily and then dealing with a divorce. If you don't believe that marrying this particular individual is the right thing for you, then you've made the correct decision to break the engagement. Just be prepared for a stormy response.

You can say something like:

> *"I've got something to tell you that I've thought long and hard about and that may come as a shock to you. I'm sorry to say that I think it would be a big mistake if we got married."*

If your fiancé answers:

> *"A big mistake? I can't believe you're saying this! What do you mean?"*

You can respond:

> *"I've done a lot of soul-searching in the past few weeks and I've come to the conclusion that our goals and values are just too different for us to have a successful marriage. I was wrong to have accepted your proposal. I'm breaking off our engagement. I'm sorry."*

If your fiancé argues:

> *"You're sorry? What am I supposed to tell my family and friends?"*

You can firmly respond:

"That is up to you, but I'm not marrying you. It will never work. It's not anyone's fault. We just weren't meant to live together happily ever after."

If your fiancé protests:

"Then why did you say yes when I proposed to you?"

You can honestly say:

"I thought I loved you enough to marry you, but I was wrong."

CHAPTER 12

Tactful Ways to Tell Your Spouse . . .

As Mary and Sal recite their wedding vows, they gaze deeply into each other's eyes. This joyous moment reinforces their feelings that they are a perfect match. Like most newlyweds, Mary and Sal assume that they are immune to the many issues that confront marriages and that once they have made their commitment to each other, the rest of their relationship will take care of itself. Statistics, however, tell us that over 50 percent of first marriages end in divorce, mostly due to lack of communication.

Do you and your spouse have frequent misunderstandings? Do you assume that each knows what the other is thinking or feeling without being told? When couples do not communicate openly, they often become frustrated, angry, and alienated. You can, however, recast angry words into assertive statements that will help your spouse understand your feelings and respond to you in a more constructive way. Here are just some of the hard things to say to your spouse and tactful ways to say them.

#64 "YOU'RE TAKING ME FOR GRANTED."

June knows that her husband, Bill, is working extra hard. To please him, she takes the kids to a sitter and spends several hours preparing a perfect meal. After arriving home an hour late, he silently gobbles down burned roast and soggy vegetables. Then, as he collapses on the couch to watch television, Jane bursts into tears and cries:

> *"You didn't even thank me for dinner! But why should you? It was ruined, and all because you were late! Everything would have been perfect if you had just arrived home on time! You always do this to me!"*

Tired after a long day at work and befuddled by his wife's temper tantrum, Bill yells back:

> *"I always do this to you? Why do you have to act like a baby when things don't go your way? You know I'm working my tail off so that you can stay home with the kids, and this is the thanks I get? All I want to do right now is relax, so just leave me alone!"*

And on that final note another exchange between June and Bill ends with both parties feeling angry, unappreciated, and resentful.

While the details surrounding arguments of this kind vary, the anger expressed is typical. Marriage experts suggest that it is best to talk openly and assertively about what bothers you before the problems grow out of proportion and sap the vitality from your marriage.

When your spouse makes you feel unappreciated or angry, you have the responsibility to express yourself—otherwise your spouse will probably just keep on making you angry. Be specific when telling your spouse how his or her actions affect you and how you would like the behavior to change.

Here is what June could say:

> *"Bill, I'm upset. When you get home late from work, it makes me feel as if I'm here simply to serve you dinner at your convenience. If you know you're going to be late, please call me."*

Here is what Bill could say:

"June, I appreciate your special dinners. But I get really frustrated when you make plans without telling me and then get mad at me because I'm working late. I feel like I'm damned if I do and damned if I don't. Can't we coordinate things a little better?"

A compromise might go like this:

"How about this? I'll call you when I know I'm going to be late, and you'll let me know ahead of time if you are planning something special for that evening. Fair enough?"

#65 "I NEED HELP AROUND THE HOUSE!"

Does your spouse leave dirty dishes in the sink and expect you to wash and put them away? Does your spouse leave a trail of dirty clothes from the bedroom to the bathroom? Are you becoming more angry and resentful because you do nearly all the housework? Most people would rather relax or go off and play than do household chores, so if the burden falls on one person's shoulders without his or her consent, resentment can quickly grow into hostility.

You may pout, grow angry, blow your stack, or emotionally withdraw from your spouse—all because you feel that you are being treated unfairly. A more constructive alternative is gently to confront your spouse with your true feelings, with the reasonable expectation that he or she will help you more.

Here's what you can say:

"I get angry when I end up doing most of the housework. I need some help around here and I expect that you can at least pick up after yourself and do your fair share. Is that asking too much?"

If your spouse growls:

"Why should I spend my free time cleaning after working all day? Anyway I mow the lawn on the weekends. What more do you want? I need my free time to relax!"

You can calmly respond:

> *"I do appreciate you mowing the lawn, but there's more to keeping up a house than that. I work all day, too, and my free time is just as valuable as yours. I need more help doing the everyday chores, such as washing dishes, vacuuming, and so on. If we each do a little at a time, then it's not like either of us has to spend hours and hours cleaning. Does that sound unreasonable?"*

If your spouse balks:

> *"This domestic stuff is such a bore, and you get so worked up about it! What's the big deal?"*

You can respond:

> *"Well, how would you feel if you did ninety-five percent of the housework and I was the one who was watching TV? Look, I don't want to argue, but if we can share the chores more evenly, I promise I'll be a lot happier and more fun to live with. How about it? Will you help me more?"*

Do not underestimate the destructive impact that an unfair distribution of housework can have on your marriage.

#66 "GET A JOB!"

This demand often follows a spouse's request for pocket money or flippant remarks about your paltry standard of living. While some people remain unemployed because they cannot find suitable work, many husbands or wives are simply lazy and would rather be supported than do their fair share.

Be pleasant, but don't mince your words when confronting a spouse who is a deadbeat. Begin with a clear statement outlining your expectations. Then follow up with questions that lead him or her to make a commitment to seek work or job training. It's fair to add some job-finding suggestions of your own. Here are some ways to motivate an idle spouse to find a job.

You can ask:

"Are you looking for work today?"

If your spouse responds:

"There are no decent jobs out there, so why should I bother looking for something that pays peanuts?"

You can answer:

"Look, I know the job market is tough right now and that you have your pride, but we must have two incomes to get by. It's that simple. Now, what can you do to find some work?"

If your spouse responds:

"I've looked in the paper and there was one decent job advertised. I called, but they had already filled the position. I never get a break! What else can I do?"

You can suggest:

"Why not call your friends and spread the word that you are looking for work? Most job openings are never advertised, and there could be a position available. You never know, you might just get lucky."

If your spouse says:

"I'm not going to beg my friends for a job. I've got my pride, you know! They'd never let me live it down."

You can counter that argument with:

"Talking to people you know about job opportunities is not begging—it's networking. It's a good way to find out about openings before someone else does. If they are true friends, they will at least give you a name of someone to talk to if they can. If you just keep talking to people, you'll find something.

If your spouse complains:

> *"Even if they told me about a job, it would probably be just as boring as my last one!"*

You can respond:

> *"The job may not be perfect, but no one says you have to stay there forever. Maybe you could get some job-training. You always wanted to learn how to use computers or even start your own business! Why not consider that alternative? It could be the start of a new career!"*

Then tell your spouse that any action he or she makes toward employment is better than no action at all. You can say:

> *"The bottom line is that you have to get a job because whatever amount of money you earn will help improve our living situation. I can't do it all alone."*

#67 "YOU NEED TO LOSE WEIGHT!"

Do you henpeck and scold your spouse for overeating or being a couch potato? Do you resort to name-calling and try to humiliate him or her into losing weight? The truth is that berating your partner for being overweight will do little more than sap his or her self-esteem.

So how can you suggest that your spouse lose weight without being a bully? First, don't make belittling personal comments or comparisons with past lovers. These kind of comments only make your spouse feel angry, depressed, and rejected. If your spouse has a serious weight problem, encourage him or her to undergo a physical exam to make sure there isn't a medical problem.

If there is no problem, then be supportive and encourage your spouse to make a personal decision to lose weight. When you hear your partner make self-deprecating remarks such as **"I hate the way I look,"** or **"I'm so fat!"** say something like:

"Well, if you feel that way, then why not do something about it? How much would you like to weigh?"

"If you lost a pound a month, that would mean that by this time next year you'd weigh twelve pounds less. Is that a realistic goal?"

"I'm sure you could lose some weight if you eat less-fattening foods. Why not cut out the cookies and brownies and see how much you can lose in a month?"

"If you feel that you need to lose weight, I'm sure that if you eat less and exercise more, you will lose weight."

If this approach does not work, then you may want to ask:

"Is there something that's bothering you and is causing you to overeat?"

"Why are you worrying so much about your weight? I think that society sets unrealistic standards for women's weight."

In the end, accepting and loving your spouse no matter how much he or she weighs will build his or her self-esteem and will act as a motivator for self-improvement. You can say:

"I'm sure losing weight will make you feel better about yourself, but I want you to know I think you're the sexiest person alive and I love you more than anyone in the world, no matter what you weigh!"

Avoid these kinds of nasty comments about weight:

"Putting on a few pounds, are we?"

"Don't you think you'd look much thinner if you didn't wear large floral designs?"

"Ah, ah! Taste makes waist!"

"I saw my old boyfriend at the store yesterday and he looks exactly the same as when we dated in high school."

"How is it that your brother stays so thin?"

"My mother was right, you have gained a lot of weight."

#68 "OUR MARRIAGE NEEDS SOME SPARK."

Did your marriage begin as a torrid love affair, but now seems uninspired and boring? Even the best relationships can fall into a romantic rut. Couples can grow tired of each other if they decrease the time and effort they put into keeping the excitement of their relationship alive. The danger of extramarital affairs and divorce increases considerably when a marriage reaches this point of indifference. Avoid tactless comments that make your spouse feel insecure about your commitment to the marriage. To recharge your love relationship, take the initiative by following these suggestions:

1. Set aside special time for yourself and your partner. Ask your spouse to spend five minutes, five hours, or a few days together without friends or family. Say something like:

"How would you like a nice five-minute back rub?"

"How about just you and me spending Saturday night together? No friends, no kids, just the two of us?"

"Let's go to that bed-and-breakfast we read about in the paper. It's been too long since we were alone together."

2. Create a romantic mood and talk about old times. It may be old-fashioned, but soft music, candlelight, flowers, little surprises, and reminiscing can really turn your partner on. You can say:

"Remember how much fun we had when we . . . ?"

"When we first met, I fell in love with you because. . . ."

"I often think of the first time we made love."

3. Change your routine of lovemaking. Seducing your spouse when he or she least expects it can be a real turn-on. Use your body language to show you want to be close and then say something like:

> *"Let's skip the dishes (TV, or whatever) for now. I want you—now!"*

> *"I love it when you. . . . It's such a turn-on. Are you in the mood for a little loving?"*

> *"What do you say we crawl into bed early tonight?"*

> *"Put the Do Not Disturb sign on our bedroom door."*

4. Stop arguing and start listening to each other. It is difficult to feel romantic when anger and resentment lurk just below the surface. Show your partner that you want to "make love, not war." Have a heart-to-heart talk about your relationship and encourage your spouse to reveal his or her feelings.

Remember to use your listening skills and rephrase what your spouse tells you without offering a defense or counterattack. Share your feelings, admit your mistakes, and say how you want things to change. Acknowledging your spouse's feelings releases anger, tension, and resentment, thus making both of you more open to romance.

Here are some examples of rephrasing what you hear to show that you are listening and understand your spouse's viewpoint:

> *"You're right. When I interrupt you, it shows I'm not listening. I'm sorry. Please continue with what you were saying."*

> *"From what you're saying, it sounds like you're disappointed in how our marriage is going. So am I. I want to work together to improve how we get along. What do you suggest?"*

> *"I never realized that I made you feel so unhappy and unappreciated when I criticized you. I was only trying to help, but I agree with what you are saying. I'm sure it*

would make you feel much better if I focused on the positive things about you."

"I'm sorry I hurt your feelings. That was a lousy thing for me to say, and I apologize. I get frustrated, too, and that's when I strike out at you. I agree that it's not right. I really want to change how we communicate."

NO MATTER WHAT YOU THINK, YOUR SPOUSE CANNOT READ YOUR MIND

Tell your spouse your wants, needs, hopes, fears, dreams, passions, and feelings. You can say:

"This is what I need from you. I need. . . ."

"This is what I want from you. I want. . . ."

"This is what I want for us."

"This is how I feel about you."

"I love you."

"I sometimes forget to tell you how much I love you."

#69 "DON'T MAKE FAMILY DECISIONS WITHOUT TALKING TO ME FIRST!"

Does your spouse buy cars or expensive items for your house without consulting you first? Do you come home and find that your favorite old chair is gone and replaced with a sofa that looks like it belongs in the Museum of Modern Art? Does he or she make major family decisions without your input?

A spouse who makes important family decisions without consulting his or her partner is a Steamroller who needs to be stopped. If you confront your domineering mate the first time it happens, then you have a chance of preventing him or her from making big decisions again without discussing it with you. Here is what you can say:

"Carl, you can't bring a dog home out of the blue and expect me to be pleased! A dog is a big responsibility that I'm not prepared to take on. You've got to take him back."

If your spouse says:

"Oh, he's so cute and he won't be much trouble. Besides, I've already put a hundred dollars down on him."

You can respond:

"A hundred dollars! We can't afford that! Sure, he's adorable, but puppies need a lot of care, and you're barely home as it is. You've got to return him and get your money back, period."

Then say:

"Look, Carl, we have to get something straight right now. I have a right to be consulted about ALL the family decisions. The next time you want to make some major purchase like a dog, car, or do anything that is going to make a change around here, let's talk about it first. Meanwhile say good-bye to Doggy!"

#70 "I'M HAVING AN AFFAIR."

First off, there is no tactful way to tell your spouse that you are having an affair, so don't even try. There are, however, three reasons why a person might consider revealing an extramarital affair.

You may feel compelled to tell your spouse about an illicit love affair to relieve your own guilt. *I don't advise it.* You might ease your mind for a short time, but the grief that it causes your spouse may quickly make you feel as bad or worse than before.

You may want to tell your spouse you are having an illicit romance as a means of getting even for his or her infidelity. *I don't advise it.* Although it may be tempting to give your spouse some of his or her own medicine, revenge is a destructive emotion and won't erase the damage.

One situation in which revealing an affair is justified is when you have decided to leave the marriage. Be direct and say:

> *"I've fallen in love with someone else, and I want a divorce."*

#71 "I'M LEAVING YOU."

Maybe getting married seemed like a good idea at the time, but things just didn't turn out the way you planned. Now your mind is made up—you want a divorce. Making the decision to end a marriage is painful, difficult, confusing, and often surrounded by guilt and fear. Many people contemplating divorce wonder how their spouse will survive without them. Here is one way of talking to yourself to help conquer this fear:

> *"I will not let fear hold me back from doing what I know is the right thing to do for me and my spouse. He (she) is a survivor, and so am I."*

Since telling a spouse you want a divorce is a highly emotional moment, script what you want to say *before* you say it. Make your statement brief and to the point, omitting any blame and anger. Be as matter-of-fact as possible. Suggest that you talk again in a few days to discuss the details of the breakup. Say that you want to remain on friendly terms, but if that isn't possible, you'll conduct the business of the divorce through your attorney. Read your "declaration of independence" aloud to yourself several times, listening to your own voice. Before you tell your spouse your plans, you can bolster your courage by saying to yourself:

> *"Getting out of this marriage is the clearest decision I've made in my life."*

You can deliver your decision in person or via the telephone. If you are not sure how your spouse is going to react, choose a public place to tell him or her your decision. Here are some ways to tell your spouse that you are through with the marriage:

*"This is difficult for me to say, but I've made up my mind.
I don't want to live with you any longer. Our marriage is
over, and I want a divorce. We need to discuss a lot of
details, and I hope we can take care of them peacefully. I
don't want to get into it right this moment, so let's talk in a
few days."*

*"I've decided that I can't stay married to you. I'm not saying
it's anyone's fault. It just didn't work out, and we both have
to share the responsibility. I'm filing for a divorce and I
hope we can work out the details in a civil way."*

Your spouse may protest and attempt to change your mind by
asking guilt-inducing questions such as:

*"What will people say? What about the children? How can
you do this to me? This is going to kill my parents!"*

Be ready to respond to manipulation by saying something like:

*"My mind is made up, I'm divorcing you. What will people
say? It's our business, so let them say whatever they want.
As far as you and the kids are concerned, all of us are going
to have to cope the best we can. It's not going to be easy for
anyone, but we'll all survive."*

DOS AND DON'TS FOR TALKING TO AN EX-SPOUSE

Do keep your social conversations light and on friendly terms.

Don't discuss visitation rights, alimony, or other personal family issues in social situations.

Do ask about your ex-spouse's family and mutual friends.

Don't bring up old arguments or past indiscretions.

Do show a willingness to forgive and forget the past.

Don't make late-night calls to your ex-spouse to talk or request favors.

Do be pleasant when you meet your ex-spouse's new partner.

Don't ask questions about your ex-spouse's personal life.

Do wish the best for your ex-spouse.

Don't gossip about your ex-spouse to mutual friends.

CHAPTER 13

Tactful Ways to Tell Your Kids . . .

Children deserve and need tactful communication just as much as adults do. Belittling comments about a child's actions, talents, or dreams can undermine the youngster's self-esteem and set the stage for underachievement. On the other hand, when adults demonstrate openness and respect for what children feel, think, and want, they can bridge the generation gap and encourage youngsters to do their best at home and in school.

#72 "I MADE A MISTAKE."

Kids know that adults are not perfect. Therefore when adults make mistakes and don't admit them, kids get confused and angry. So, when you make a blunder with your child, don't try to justify your behavior by using the excuse that you are an adult. Admitting your mistakes sets a positive example and makes your actions consistent with your words. It also shows that you respect the child's right to have feelings and opinions.

Here are some typical examples of tactless and tactful ways to talk to your child about your mistakes:

Tactless Way to Talk	Tactful Way to Talk
"How many times have I told you, don't contradict me!"	*"Why don't you agree with what I've said?"*
"I don't make mistakes."	*"You're right, I goofed."*

"If I hurt your feelings, that's too damn bad.

"There's no way that I could be wrong."

"That was a dumb thing to say. I apologize."

"You're right and I was wrong."

#73 "YOU SHOULD HAVE DONE IT MY WAY!"

Well-meaning parents and teachers may think they are helping kids avoid failure by telling them what to do, when to do it, and how to do it. Nothing is more demoralizing to a child's enthusiasm than to hear an adult's endless criticism of how something "should have been done."

Replace criticism and browbeating with praise that separates the child's efforts from the results. The strategy is to promote your child's persistence as a means to achieving his or her goals. Here is an example of how to reinforce your child's self-esteem and motivation even if he or she did not "make the team."

For example, you can say to your child:

"I want to congratulate you for trying out for the basketball team."

If your child says:

"Yeah, but I didn't make it! So why congratulate me?"

You can respond:

"Hey, look, the competition was tough. I'm sorry you didn't make the team, but I'm proud that you decided to give it a shot anyway. That shows self-confidence!"

If your child says:

"What good is confidence if I didn't make the team? That's what it's all about."

You can respond:

"Sure you wanted to make the team, but it's about more than that. It's also about persistence. If you want something badly enough—whatever it is—you'll keep working at it until you get it."

#74 "YOU NEVER DO ANYTHING RIGHT!"

Adult input continuously reinforces a child's behavior and self-image. If the child constantly hears how bad, dumb, and careless he or she is, it doesn't take long for the child to see himself or herself in this way too. By praising children 80 percent of the time and criticizing them only 20 percent you can boost their self-esteem.

The strategy is to catch your kids doing something right. When you see positive behavior, identify it aloud and praise it *without* adding on a critical zinger such as, ***"That was good, but. . . ."*** Here are several examples:

"Thanks for taking out the trash without me asking you. I really appreciate you pitching in around here."

"It might seem like a little thing to you, but I appreciate it when you remember to wipe your feet when you come in the door. It really helps keep the house clean. Thanks."

"You really impressed me with your performance today! It takes a lot of nerve to go up on stage and give a speech. How did it feel to be out there in front of all those people?"

"I think you deserve a lot of credit for admitting that you broke the window, especially when all your friends ran away."

"I'm proud of you for standing up for what you think is right even if your friends laughed at you. That took courage on your part!"

"I'm happy to see that you're finishing your homework without me standing over you."

#75 "FINISH YOUR HOMEWORK!"

Homework can be a frustrating and time-consuming nightly chore for both kids and parents alike. The coddling parent feels compelled to check every detail of each assignment, while the unmotivated youngster tries to make as little effort as possible. Some lazy kids even get their parents to complete their assignments for them. Another common homework scenario ends with the frustrated child in tears as the irritated parent yells, ***"You're not trying! Now do it again!"***

One way parents can decrease homework hassles is to become less involved in the details of each assignment. The strategy is to establish a homework routine, be available but not hover, delegate responsibility, encourage independence, and provide praise and positive feedback. Here is a five-step plan to get your child started on his or her homework and put the responsibility on his or her shoulders, not yours:

STEP 1: ESTABLISH A DAILY ROUTINE

Begin homework early and in a quiet place, such as the child's room. While it is the child's responsibility to complete homework assignments, it is the parents' responsibility to provide a quiet, well-lit place with necessary supplies. The kitchen table is *not* the best place for a child to complete his or her homework, because there are too many distractions. Agree on a time for homework, turn off the television, and get started. Establishing a routine is half the battle.

Plan homework over the week. Start the homework session on Monday with a five-minute overview of all assignments for that evening and week. Have your child make a chart and list each assignment and its due date, and estimate about how long each assignment will take to complete. This is tricky because elementary and junior high school students typically underestimate the amount of time it takes to complete an assignment. Also, set a time to quit, and stick to it.

You can help your child increase the accuracy in his or her time estimates by asking:

> *"Is this a reasonable amount of time to complete the assignment?"*

"Have you thought about everything you need to do to complete this assignment from start to finish, including organizing your supplies, reading the instructions, checking over the work for accuracy, and making it neat?"

STEP 2: BE AVAILABLE TO HELP IF YOU ARE NEEDED— BUT DON'T HOVER

Instead of watching over your child's shoulder as he or she starts the assignments, get him or her started by saying:

"First read the instructions and tell me what they are asking you to do."

If your child gets confused and says:

"I don't get it. What am I supposed to do?"

You can say:

"Well, let's read the directions aloud together and figure it out. What is your first step?"

STEP 3: HELP WITH THE FIRST EXAMPLE OR BEGIN THE EXERCISE

Ask your child to work out the first example or begin the assignment. For example, you can say:

"Let's try the first math exercise together and see if you've got the right idea."

"What might be a fun way to start writing a ghost story? Any ideas?"

"How could you use the first word on your spelling list in a sentence?"

"Since your science report is on the 'endangered species,' in which volumes of the encyclopedia might you find some information to get you started?"

STEP 4: OFFER PRAISE AND POSITIVE FEEDBACK

Once your child understands the assignment and has started, provide brief, but positive feedback. For example, you can say:

"You've done the first three math exercises perfectly! Good job! Let's try one word problem before I leave the rest to you. Do you have any questions? Is there anything you're not sure how to do? Keep up the good work!"

"I really like the beginning of your story. I can't wait to read what happens next! Let me know when you're finished."

"You're on the right track. Way to go. Now work right on through to the end of the assignment and you'll be finished."

"If you get stuck on one part, then move on to the next. Many times you can answer your own questions or work out the problem as long as you keep plugging away."

Avoid criticizing too much, setting unrealistic expectations, or getting bogged down in the details. Instead encourage neatness, accuracy, and creativity. Once your child successfully starts the assignment, leave the room and let him or her work alone.

STEP 5: PERIODICALLY CHECK ON YOUR CHILD'S PROGRESS

After a half hour or so check in and see how your child is progressing with the assignment. If he or she is making good headway with the work, then offer quiet praise and positive feedback. Don't demand perfection or be overenthusiastic. Simply smile, put your hand on your child's shoulder, and say:

"You're doing fine. Keep up the good work!"

Then leave the room and let your child continue working. If your child protests, *"This is too hard!"* or *"I can't"* or *"I'm too tired to think of anything"* do not finish the work for him or her. Suggest that your child take a five-minute break (no television!) to stretch, get a healthful snack, and a breath of fresh air. Then, back at the desk, briefly offer some help to break the mental logjam. If after twenty minutes of assistance your child remains stuck, then you can say:

> *"I know this is hard for you, but if you really feel you've given it your best shot tonight, put it away for now and go on to another one of your homework assignments. Then tomorrow before class I want you to ask your teacher to please explain this assignment to you again."*

If your child is frequently frustrated with the homework in a particular subject, contact his or her teacher to discuss the problem and possible solutions.

#76 "I DON'T LIKE YOUR FRIENDS!"

While parents have a right to be concerned about who their children socialize with, dictating who is or is not a suitable companion for a teenager will surely lead to conflict. Before you chastise your teenager's friend, ask yourself why your feelings are so negative about him or her. Is your disapproval based purely on appearance or is it based on genuine facts? Is the friend rude or overly secretive? Is he or she too wild or too old for your child? Do you suspect that he or she is involved in illegal or undesirable activities? Are your negative feelings directed more at the friend's parents or family lifestyle? Whatever your reason for disapproving of the friend, *how* you convey your feelings to your youngster is probably more important than *what* you actually say.

For example, if you feel the friend is rude because he walks into your house without even glancing at you, you can say to your teenager:

> *"Whenever your friend Tom comes here to see you, he acts as if I'm not even here. It's rude for him to come into my*

*house and not even say, 'Hello, how are you?' I don't dislike
Tom, but I will pretty soon if he keeps acting as if I don't
exist! Would you please tell him that I'd like to be treated
with more courtesy."*

Maybe you feel that the friend's behavior is a bad influence on
your teenager. You can talk about your concerns with your
youngster, but choose a time other than when he or she is head-
ing out the door. If you simply forbid your child to see the
friend, you will no doubt instigate an argument and get the
opposite results. If you take a less dictatorial position, you may
get your child to consider your feelings and maybe compromise.
First you can encourage your teenager to tell you about his or
her friend by asking:

"Which classes are you in together?"

*"What do you like to do together when you're not in
school?"*

"Does he/she have any special talents?"

"Have you met your friend's family? What are they like?"

Listen carefully for specific information and ask follow-up questions, but do not make it sound like an interrogation. Then
share your observations and concerns with your child. You can
say:

*"You might find this hard to understand, but I don't like
you hanging out with Jessie because. . . ."*

*"I'm concerned that there is no adult at Carmen's house
until well after eight p.m. If you want to study together,
why don't you ask her to come over here?"*

*"Do you understand why I'm worried about the time you
spend with Jerome when he comes in here smelling like a
brewery?"*

Even if you are opposed to your child spending time with this particular friend, consider that most teenagers usually do what they want despite their parents' objections. The most useful strategy you can employ to influence your child's behavior is to promote a receptive atmosphere where you can talk openly.

You make the rules for your child. If you are absolutely opposed to him or her spending time with an undesirable peer, then say calmly and firmly:

> *"Look, I don't like this guy. What you've told me just reinforces my feelings about him. Ever since you've been hanging around with him, your grades have dropped and you've picked up an attitude that is getting hard to take. I think he is bad news and headed for trouble. If you keep hanging out with him, you'll be in trouble too. Please do me a big favor. I want you to steer clear of him and spend your free time with your other friends."*

If your child says:

> *"He's my friend and you can't stop me!"*

You can respond:

> *"Maybe I can't stop you, but you know how I feel about him, and I expect you to do as I ask."*

#77 "DON'T DO IT."

Once children reach puberty, their curiosity about sex grows, and so does their desire to experiment. Some parents mistakenly believe that keeping their teenager ignorant about sex assures his or her innocence, but nothing could be farther from the truth. Kids are already learning about sex from the movie screen, television, and their friends, although the information is not always accurate.

Even if parents promote abstinence, they can still encourage open discussion about sexual values. Here are a few thought-provoking questions about sex and love that you can discuss with your teenager:

"I was reading an article about kids your age who are sexually active. What do you think about these teenagers having babies? Do you think these young people are doing the right thing?"

"I understand there are some sex-education classes in your school. I'd like to hear about the topics they are covering."

"What can you do if someone puts pressure on you to have sex?"

"What do you know about how a baby is conceived?"

"What do you know about birth control?"

"What do you know about preventing sexually transmitted diseases?"

Whether parents are dictatorial, puritanical, manipulative, or open-minded, they have good reason to be concerned with the sexual values and habits of their teenagers. Precisely how parents communicate their own sexual values to their children is more important than the actual words they say about sex and sexual values. As the old saying goes, "A picture is worth a thousand words."

#78 "YOU'VE GOT A DRUG PROBLEM."

Every parent's worst nightmare is the thought that his or her child is on drugs. Yet many naive parents believe that their teenager will be immune from this scourge. Denying that a youngster may have a drug or alcohol problem just makes facing the issue that much more difficult. The question is, what is the difference between experimentation and drug addiction?

Drug- and alcohol-addiction experts recommend that teachers and parents alike confront young people who they believe are using drugs or alcohol. Clues of drug or alcohol abuse may include finding drugs or drug paraphernalia in your teenager's room, missing prescription pills from the family medicine cabinet, missing money or items of value, erratic or hostile behavior, lethargy, hyperactivity, lying, excuses, poor school performance, job loss, desperate pleas for money, or associating with people involved with drugs or illegal activities.

There are no easy answers to teenage drug or alcohol addiction. If you believe that your child is on drugs, you can confront him or her with the evidence, and be prepared to respond to denials, accusations, and empty promises.

For example, say to your teenager:

"I found liquor, drug paraphernalia, cocaine, and marijuana in your room. I think we've got a serious problem, and we are going to talk about it right now."

If your kid says:

"What are you doing snooping in my room? I told you to stay out of my things! You don't respect my privacy!"

Then you can say:

"I can understand why you feel that way, but it doesn't change the facts that I found booze and drugs in your room. What do you have to say about that?"

If your kid tries to brush it off by saying:

"Everyone does it, it's no big deal."

Then you can set the record straight and say:

"You may think that it's no big deal, but I disagree with you. I think it is a big deal."

If your kid says:

"You drank when you were a teenager, so why can't I?"

Then you can respond:

"Maybe I did, but that doesn't make it right. Besides, anyone your age drinking hard liquor and using hard drugs is

headed for serious trouble. I won't let you continue doing that. I think that you need help."

If your kid says:

"You're so old-fashioned. I don't drink or use drugs any more than anyone else. Anyway I was just experimenting."

Then you can say:

"That may be true, but it is against the law for you to drink or use drugs. If you are caught, you will go to court and maybe to jail. Anyway it seems like anyone who has this much stuff must use it a lot. I think you've got a serious problem, and we are going to do something about it."

#79 "SHAPE UP OR SHIP OUT!"

Living together peacefully requires compromises from parents and children. Parents need to respect their teenagers' privacy and growing desire for independence. At the same time, adolescents need to understand their parents' concerns too.

Even though you and your teenagers may have conflicting values and opinions, it is you, the parent, who must set reasonable limits that can be enforced. Rather than using empty threats when teenagers break the rules or misbehave, you need to find sensible ways of dealing with the problems.

You can say:

"As long as you are living in this house, we expect you to. . . . If you have a problem with that, let's talk about it."

"I understand that your friends get to stay out later, but our rules are that on a school night you be home by. . . ."

"When you live on your own, you can do as you please, but until that time you'll have to respect our wishes and rules."

"Just because we call the shots here doesn't mean that we can't negotiate a little. Let's talk."

When your teenager lives up to your expectations, reinforce the positive behavior with some additional privileges or a reward. You can say:

> *"We are happy with the ways you have been contributing around the house and sticking to the rules, so we'd like to talk to you about where you'd like some additional privileges."*

#80 "YOUR FATHER (MOTHER) AND I ARE GETTING A DIVORCE."

The breaking up of a family is unquestionably one of the most stressful events children and parents face. Loving parents want to protect their child from the harsh realities of divorce, but silence only raises the child's suspicion and creates more anxiety. After all, the child has lived with the parents' mutual tension and hostility for years, so it will do little good for the parents to hide the fact that they are separating.

According to most family counseling experts, it is best for both parents to speak to the child at the same time without going into all the gory details that went into the decision. Be straightforward, honest, and talk on a level that your child will understand. You can say something like:

> *"When your father (mother) and I got married, we loved each other very much. We were so happy when you were born, and you are still our greatest joy—that will never change. Everything in our family was okay for a while, but then your father (mother) and I started to argue a lot. Now we both feel very unhappy living with each other. Even though we both feel sad, it's best that your father (mother) and I get divorced and don't live together anymore."*

Never burden your child with your suffering, ask them to take sides, or present all the details that went into making the decision. Make it absolutely clear that your child is not the cause of the divorce by saying something like:

> *"We want you to understand that you did not cause this to happen. The reason we are getting a divorce is because*

your father (mother) and I are unhappy and do not want to be married to each other anymore."

Emphasize that neither parent is abandoning the child. Say:

"Even though we won't be living together anymore, your father (mother) and I will always love you, be your parents, and see you. You will always be our child no matter what happens."

When you talk to your child about divorce, focus on his or her needs and be ready to answer many questions such as:

"What will happen to me?"

"Who am I going to live with?"

"Where will I live?"

"Who will feed me and take care of me if I get sick?"

"Will I still get to see Grandma and Grandpa?"

"What should I tell my friends and teacher?"

You may not know all the answers to all your child's questions, but say that you will do your best to help him or her handle each situation as it arises. Be prepared for a variety of emotional responses from your child. A six-year-old may ask straightforward questions that go to the heart of the matter, while a teenager's stony silence might be followed by angry outbursts and accusations.

Experts advise divorcing parents to accept without argument their child's strong reactions and feelings. You can say:

"I understand why you are angry and upset, but no matter how angry and upset you are, we are still your parents and we love you."

Some older children—especially teens—may not want to talk openly about their feelings. Exerting pressure on your child to talk probably won't do anything but worsen the situation. It is better to back off and say:

> *"I know this divorce is hard for you—it's hard for all of us. I want you to know that your feelings are very important to us, and we understand that you need time to think about what is going on."*

> *"No matter what you might be wishing, your father (mother) and I are not getting back together again."*

If after a reasonable time your child still does not want to discuss the matter with you or does not accept that the divorce is taking place, you may wish to arrange a consultation for you and your child with a professional counselor.

#81 "THIS IS MY NEW FRIEND."

The first meeting between your child and your prospective partner is very important and will set the tone for the relationship. You can make your child feel more comfortable sharing you with a potential mate by first introducing him or her as a "friend." Plan an activity your child enjoys and that you can talk about afterward, such as a trip to the zoo, park, or sporting event.

You can introduce your child and friend by saying:

> *"Dean, I'd like you to meet my new friend, Kim. Kim, this is my son, Dean. I've told Kim a lot about you, and she's been wanting to meet you. I've invited Kim to come with us to the park. Kim is an animal lover, just like you! She has two cats! Dean, why don't you tell Kim about your pets while we walk to the park."*

Your child will have a positive first impression of your new friend if they chat and have fun. Gradually increase the time the three of you spend together so that everyone can get to know each other better and become comfortable. Keep in mind that both your child and your friend will want your undivided attention. Balance the amount of time you spend talking to each of them so that neither one feels excluded.

Encourage your child and new friend to carry on an independent conversation by excusing yourself from the situation for a few minutes. You can help your new friend to converse with your child if you tell him or her some of your child's interests and activities. Your friend can share his or her interests, too, and can ask questions. Here are some examples:

"Do you want to hear a funny story about one of my cats?"

"How did you decide what to name your hamster?"

"What is your favorite subject in school?"

"I hear you're a big baseball fan. Who do you think is going to come in first place this year?"

"Your dad told me that you are taking dance lessons. That sounds like fun. I'm taking dance lessons, too, because I love to dance!"

#82 "I'M GETTING REMARRIED."

It is natural for children—no matter what the age—to be upset or wary when a divorced parent decides to date and eventually remarry. Describing your fiancé as a "new" mother or father can trigger an adverse reaction from your child, including questions of loyalty to his or her other biological parent and many of the fears associated with the original breakup of the family.

Be patient and expect some caution on the part of your child. After all, it is a lot to ask a child to accept a divorce, new living arrangements, new adult relationships, remarriages, and probably new siblings. Easing into these changes and new relationships can decrease the chances of your child rejecting a potential spouse. You can say:

"No one will ever replace your father (mother), but I am very fond of . . . , and someday we will probably get mar-

ried. When that happens, he (she) will live with us and be part of our family."

"Sonia, I want you to get to know Evon better because someday she and I may get married."

"Felix and I are talking about getting married. How do you feel about that?"

"What do you think about the idea of Sue and me getting married?"

"Toby and I have decided to get married. We love each other very much and want to live together with you. Some things in your and my daily lives will change, and I know you will probably have a lot of questions. We'll try to answer them the best we can. The main thing to remember is that you are still the most important person in my life, and I'll always be here for you."

#83 "GRANDMA'S GONE FOREVER."

It is natural for parents to want to protect their children from the pain and grief that accompany the loss of a loved one. Child psychologists, however, suggest that parents encourage their children to express their fears and feelings about the death openly. Experts also advise parents to give their children a reassuring, warm hug accompanied by an honest and simple explanation of what happened instead of confusing them with euphemisms such as *"Grandma has gone to sleep forever."*

For example, if a grandparent dies, a parent can say something like:

"You know that Grandma has died and we won't see her anymore. You loved Grandma very much, didn't you?"

"All of us are sad that Grandma died and won't be with us anymore."

"Grandma told me before she died that she loved all of us very much."

"We are all going to miss Grandma, aren't we?"

Your child may ask many difficult questions about death. In this case you can say:

"There are many things about death that we don't understand, and I can't answer all your questions, but I'll do my best."

"Sometimes people die and we just don't know why."

"Once a person dies, he or she can never come back to life again."

"It is natural for a very old person like Grandma to die quietly. That is the best way to end a long and happy life."

DOS AND DON'TS FOR TACTFUL CONVERSATIONS WITH KIDS

Don't say, *"I'm older and wiser."*
Do say, *"I disagree with you, but tell me why you think that."*
Don't say, *"Because I said so, that's why!"*
Do say, *"You know the rules, and I'm holding you to them."*
Don't say, *"Go figure it out for yourself."*
Do say, *"I'll try to explain it to you."*
Don't say, *"When I was your age, I. . . ."*
Do say, *"I want to know how you see the situation."*
Don't say, *"You'll never amount to anything!"*
Do say, *"You can achieve anything you desire—if you want it badly enough!"*
Don't say, *"You shouldn't feel like that!"*
Do say, *"Tell me why you feel that way."*
Don't say, *"I told you so!"*
Do say, *"We all make mistakes. The idea is to learn from them."*
Don't say, *"Why can't you be like your sister (brother)?"*
Do say, *"You and your sister (brother) each have your own talents, and I love both of you very much."*
Don't say, *"You're just like your father (mother)!"*
Do say, *"You are a unique individual!"*
Don't say, *"How could you do this to me?"*
Do say, *"You are responsible for your actions—how they affect others as well as yourself."*
Don't say, *"If you know what's good for you, you'll do as we say."*
Do say, *"We love you and even if we don't agree with you, we'll support your decision."*

CHAPTER 14

Tactful Ways to Tell Your Parents . . .

"Sure I love my parents, but when they treat me like a thirteen-year-old kid, it drives me crazy."

Do your parents still talk to you like a teenager even though you're an adult? Do they constantly tell you what's best for you, the "right" way to think, how to spend your money, and how you ought to live your life? Do you push each other's "emotional buttons," make thoughtless remarks, and get into petty arguments that leave everyone frustrated, hurt, and angry?

If you said *yes* to these questions, you are using the same adult-to-child patterns you did as a youngster. You haven't yet graduated to an adult-to-adult level of communication with your parents. You can't change your parents, but you can change *how* you communicate with them. The following entries demonstrate how to break the cycle of adult-to-child communication and can lead to more open and rewarding conversations with your parents. The basic strategies are: to listen, ask for clarification, consider their suggestions, make your own decisions, and above all keep your sense of humor!

#84 "QUIT TREATING ME LIKE A KID!"

Since you will always be your parents' child no matter how old you are, accept the fact that they will sometimes disapprove of your behavior, lifestyle, or decisions, just as they did when you were growing up. When your parents berate your plans or dreams, you don't have to defend yourself immediately. Keep silent, take some deep breaths, and make an effort to distance yourself emotionally from their critical comments. In other words, become less sensitive to their disapproval and don't respond when your parents "push your buttons." At this point your strategy is to listen and then ask for clarification.

Your parents may tell you what to do because it fulfills *their* need for involvement, not because you need their advice. Rather than fight with your parents, consider this strategy: Give in a little in order to get your way. "Giving in" in this case means showing a sincere willingness to listen to, but not necessarily accept, their advice. Asking for clarification and listening indicates flexibility and receptivity on your part, and this alone often fulfills your parents' desire to be intimately involved in your life. For example, if your mother makes a nasty comment about your appearance, you can say:

> *"What is it about my hair that you don't care for? The color? the length? the style? What exactly bothers you about it?"*

If your mother says:

> *"Well, to begin with it's so long, I can't see your eyes! And dyeing it red! Most women would give anything to have your natural blond hair!"*

You can respond with:

> *"I see. Anything else?"*

Even if your parent's criticism becomes even more intense, remain cool and calm. Remember, you don't have to defend, agree, or comply—all you have to do is listen. Use reflective listening skills and rephrase what your mother said. This shows you are listening and considering her point. Here are examples of reflective listening:

> *"Mom, if I understand you correctly, you'd like my hair better if it was shorter in front and closer to its natural color? Did I hear that right?"*

"Mother, let me see if I understand what you are saying. You're suggesting that if I cut my bangs and change my hair color back to blond, I'd look more attractive? Is that what you mean?"

This gives your parent the opportunity to say:

"Yes, that's exactly what I mean. You're finally listening to me."

"No, that's not what I mean exactly. Let me explain it this way."

Next, think about your parents' advice and opinions instead of rejecting their ideas immediately. Show a willingness to consider the alternative and try to agree with at least one point they have made. Here are several examples of what you can say to show your parents that you are considering their viewpoint:

"Mom, I'll think about what you've said."

"I appreciate you telling me that I had beautiful hair. I never knew you felt that way."

"You may be right about. . . ."

"I never looked at it in quite that way."

Strive for Respect, Not Approval

When you and your parents disagree over hairstyles, lifestyle choices, family values, or emotional issues, make it a point to say that you are not seeking their agreement or approval. However, it is fair to expect them to respect your right to your opinions and point of view. To emphasize this, you can say:

"It's obvious that we disagree about . . . , but you are entitled to your opinion, and of course so am I."

If your parent insists on badgering you about a sensitive topic, simply say:

> *"I'm really here to spend some pleasant time with you, not to fight. Do you mind if we talk about something else right now?"*

#85 "DON'T TELL ME HOW TO RUN MY LIFE!"

The next time your overbearing parents attempt to organize your life, remember that self-control and listening are the key words to coping with them. No matter what they say or do to undermine your independence and self-esteem, throwing a temper tantrum or fighting back only reinforces their view that you are immature and incapable of making intelligent decisions. On the other hand, if you ask questions and listen for the main issues that bother them, your parents will respond in a different manner.

When you ask your parents for advice, you will:

- Fulfill their parental need to nurture and coach you.
- Give them the opportunity to voice their concerns or clarify their objections.
- Receive the benefit of their experience.
- Have the opportunity to find points of agreement.
- Have the opportunity to calm down and keep from losing your temper.
- Have time to formulate a tactful response.
- Remain free to consider an alternative view without being forced into having a fight or making a decision.

For example, you can say:

> *"Mom, Dad, I'm seriously thinking about quitting my post office job and going into business for myself. This is something I've always wanted, and I'm determined to make it work. What do you think?"*

If your parents respond:

"Quit your job and start a business in this economy!? Are you nuts? Do you know how many people want a secure government job like yours? What about your pension and health insurance? You need your head examined! You're not going to quit that job!"

You can say:

"I know you have my best interests at heart, and I'm listening to what you are saying. Your points about the weak economy and job security are well taken. But I'm curious, what would you do if you were working at a job for more than ten years that bored you to tears and you had more ambitious career goals?"

If your parents respond (perhaps a bit more slowly):

"Well, to begin with, I wouldn't quit one job before I had something to replace it with."

You can respond:

"I agree with that advice, and that's why I've been baking and selling cakes and pies in my spare time and saving the money I earned. The problem is, I can't keep up with the demand! Business is too good! What would you do if you were in my position?"

If your parents reveal their fears by saying:

"We're not sure, but starting a business seems very risky. We'd hate to see you fail and lose everything. If you like to bake so much, why not get a job in a bakery?"

You can acknowledge their concerns and suggestions by saying:

"I appreciate your concern about me changing jobs. You're right. It is a risky thing to do, and I'll think carefully about your advice. Maybe I can find someone who has a bakery and wants a partner. That's an idea worth pursuing."

Your parents may respond more optimistically by saying:

"Well, at least that way you'd be sharing some of the risk. So you're not going to quit your job in the post office, are you?"

You can resist another of their attempts to control your life by saying:

"Mom, Dad, I want you to know that I value your opinions even though we don't agree all the time. You've brought up some good points, and I want to think about them before I make any decision. But please remember, when it comes down to the final decision, I'll do what I think is best."

Many overbearing parents will back off once you give them an opportunity to offer their input and you show a willingness to listen and consider their suggestions. Keep in mind that if your decision goes against your parents' advice, they may still disapprove—and let you know it. If, however, you are determined to take charge of your own life, build your self-esteem, and fulfill your dreams, then you have probably made the right decision. After all, you know what's best for you, and in the end your parents will probably support any decision that makes you a happier and more fulfilled individual.

#86 "I'D LIKE TO BORROW SOME MONEY."

Asking your parents to loan you money requires tact because frequently there are varying attitudes surrounding this sensitive subject. No matter what your parents' attitudes are about money, you can be sure that they will react negatively to an insensitive request for a loan.

Before you barge into your parents' house and ask for a loan, get a sense of how they feel about their fiscal condition and outlook.

Never underestimate their concern for their own financial security. You may be unaware of financial obligations, medical problems, or even a dream vacation that require large expenditures. Avoid asking for a loan if you sense that your parents feel insecure about their own financial future. To open the topic of their financial security, you can ask:

"How are those stocks of yours doing?"

"Now that you and mom are retired, do you find that living on your interest income is okay?"

"How did those investments you made last year pan out?"

"Do you have any big investment plans coming up?"

If your folks ask you the reason for your sudden interest in their financial situation, be honest. If your goal is to buy a house, for example, you can say:

"I want to buy a house, and I was wondering how you feel about the possibility of loaning me some money for a down payment? The thing is, I don't want to put any extra financial pressure on you, so that's why I asked how things are going."

Be ready to tell your parents how much you want to borrow. Assure them that their investment is safe and worthwhile. Then explain to them on what terms you will pay it back. You can say:

"I've been saving to buy a house for the last five years, and I just recently found the perfect place. The problem is that I need about five thousand dollars more for a down payment. If you're willing, I'd like to borrow about that amount and pay it back to you with interest over a period of five years."

If your parents reject your request, then just accept it. *Never* say:

"Ah, come on, you and mom can afford it."

"I can't believe you're still mad about that five hundred dollars I never paid you back."

"Nina's dad loaned her twice that amount of money to buy a house, so why can't you float me a loan too?"

Treat a Family Loan Like Any Other Business Arrangement

Family loans often run into trouble because the agreements are unwritten or sloppy. Insist on a written agreement that clearly spells out everyone's obligations. This shows that you approach the loan in a businesslike way and that you are serious about keeping your end of the bargain. And if you respect your parents and value your relationship with them, don't conveniently forget to send your monthly check or start falling behind on your payments. In other words, never ask your parents for a loan if what you really want is a gift.

#87 "MY MARRIAGE IS OVER."

Most parents want their children to be happily married, so telling your parents that you are getting a divorce is as painful and difficult for them as it is for you. Expect your parents to feel upset, sad, angry, guilty, relieved, humiliated, and disappointed when they hear the news. Be calm and straightforward when you tell them your decision. You can say something like:

"Mom and Dad, I have something important to tell you about Susie and me that will probably upset you. We're getting a divorce because we've both been unhappy for a long time. We've talked to a marriage counselor for the past several months to try to work out some of our differences, but it just hasn't done any good. We've both agreed that it is best for everyone concerned that we get a divorce."

Your parents, however, may feel that you are making a mistake and might try to change your mind. They may try to pressure you into staying married. Here are some common questions or comments that you may face from parents and ways to answer them.

If your parents say:

"We thought you two were so happy. Surely the two of you can work it out."

You can say:

"I know this is hard for you to accept, but we're getting a divorce because we don't love each other anymore."

If your parents say:

"But what about the kids? How can you do this to them? What are you going to tell them? Where are they going to live? Are we still going to get to see them?"

You can say:

"I understand your concern for our kids. Obviously we're concerned, too, but living in a home with two parents fighting all the time isn't a great way to grow up. It's not going to be easy on any of us, but we'll cope. We'll work out the living arrangements with our lawyers. And, yes, of course you'll get to see them. They'll always be your grandchildren. Nothing will change that."

If your parents say:

"How can you do this to us after all we have done for you two? You're just a couple of spoiled brats! In our day people didn't get divorced at the drop of a hat!"

You can say:

"I can understand why you feel so upset. We're upset, too, but we've made our decision to get a divorce, and that's final. Believe me, we feel badly that our marriage did not work out, but this is reality, and we're dealing with it. Everyone is going to be okay, but it's going to take time."

Even though your parents will probably feel terrible about your divorce, they may support your decision and say something like:

"We're sad that you two couldn't work it out, but we've known for a long time that neither of you have been happy. You have to do what you think is best. Let us know if there is anything we can do to help. We still love both of you."

#88 "DON'T MARRY HER!"

Your widowed father recently met a single woman he likes, and they are talking about getting married. Naturally your father and his new friend are enamored of each other, but you're not so sure their getting married is such a good idea. In fact you think that this infatuation is clouding your dad's better judgment.

Most adult children want to see their single parent happily remarried. But what do you say if you feel strongly that your parent's fiancé is the wrong person for him or her to marry? Is it your place to voice your opinion with the hope that your parent will call the wedding off before it's too late? How do you tactfully tell your mother or father that you think marrying this person would be a disaster? Will your initial disapproval get a new step-relationship off to a bad start?

Questioning a parent's choice of a potential spouse requires a great deal of tact and an open mind. Even adult children often feel a flood of anger, sadness, jealousy, and a host of other emotions. Rather than blurt out, *"What would Mom think!"* or some other guilt-provoking statement, let your doubts about the matchup come out more subtly. For example, you can respond with comments or questions, such as:

"I don't know her well enough to say if I think it's a good idea or not. My first impression is that you ought to give it more time."

"To be honest, I'm surprised that you are even talking about marriage, since you've only been dating each other for a month."

"Are you sure she's the right one for you? I didn't think she was really your type."

"She's nice, but her lifestyle seems so different from yours. Are you sure you two would be compatible?"

"What's the hurry? Why not give it some more time and see how things progress?"

If your parent does decide to remarry, remember that:

- It is his or her decision. Accept it and respect it.
- It is tactless and hurtful to compare the new stepparent to your biological parent. Every person has some good qualities.
- Your support, enthusiasm, cooperation, and flexibility will help your parent's remarriage succeed.
- You do not have to love a new stepparent right away, but your consideration, courtesy, and respect are a must.
- Give your new step-relationship time to develop trust and love.

#89 "I'M MARRYING SOMEONE OF ANOTHER FAITH."

Most parents raise their children within the framework of a particular religion because that is how they grew up. Whether you were raised Christian, Jewish, or Muslim, your religion provides your family with security, heritage, and values in a fast-changing world. Parents usually expect that their children will follow the same religious path and marry someone of the same faith.

If you choose to marry someone from another faith, be prepared for family conflict. Your parents and other family members may see you as a traitor who rejects not only their religion but all their values. While this reaction may seem extreme, your ability to present your decision tactfully will help your parents and family understand and respect your new spouse.

Your strategy for a smooth interfaith marriage is to strive for your family's tolerance and respect, but not agreement. Here are some typical questions and comments that you may face, and tactful ways to respond. Rephrase what you hear and show you are listening by asking follow-up questions to help build a bridge across this extremely delicate area of family relations.

If your parent says:

"You're turning your back on your family. How can you do this to us?"

You can say:

"I understand you are upset, but why would marrying someone from a different religion mean that I was turning my back on my family?"

If your parent says:

"Which religious holidays are you going to celebrate?"

You should be direct and sincere, saying something along the lines of:

"We're going to celebrate both of our religion's holidays (or whatever decision you have reached)."

If your parent says:

"You're going to raise your children in our religion, aren't you?"

You can say:

"Not exactly. We've agreed to raise our children in a family that incorporates both religions."

If your parent says:

"What are we supposed to tell our friends?"

You can say:

"I understand this is difficult for you and I'm sure some of your friends might disapprove. But can you explain to me what they have to do with our decision?"

If your parent says:

> *"As far as I'm concerned you're a disgrace to our family
> and I never want to see you again."*

You can say:

> *"I know you are upset. You don't have to agree with my
> decision, but all I'm asking is for you to be a little more
> tolerant and give us a chance to make it work."*

#90 "I'M GAY."

Heterosexuality is more than an expectation to most parents—it
is an assumption. As a result, learning that a son or daughter is
gay may come as quite a shock. If you are a homosexual, how
and when your parents find out about your sexual orientation
can make the difference between them accepting you and rejecting you. For example, if you "come out" at your parents'
fiftieth wedding anniversary party by dancing slowly with your
lover, you are certainly going to offend your parents, family,
and their friends. On the other hand, if you tactfully reveal
your sexuality in private, then your parents may be more tol-
erant of your lifestyle. Here are some examples of how to tell
your parents about your sexual orientation:

> *"You may have already guessed, but I want you to know for
> sure that I'm gay."*

> *"I want to tell you something about myself that may upset
> you. I'm gay and I've been living with another man (or
> woman) for many years."*

> *"You know my friend Sarah? Well, she's really more than a
> friend. We've been lovers for years and I felt it was time to
> tell you directly that I'm gay."*

Your parents may respond with shock, confusion, or anger. Be
prepared for what may seem like tactless questions, comments,
or downright hostility.

For instance, if your parents say:

"You were married and have kids! How could you possibly be gay?"

You can respond:

"I understand that you are surprised. It's true that I was married and have two kids, but that doesn't change the fact that I'm gay."

If your parents try to make you feel guilty by saying:

"Oh, this is just great! How could you do this to us?"

You can answer:

"I hope you don't feel that I'm trying to punish you in some way. It's not a reflection on you; it's just the way I am."

If your parents become irate and say:

"No son of ours could be gay. We don't believe it! Get out of our house. We never want to talk to you again!"

You can stand tall and say:

"I understand that you are upset and angry. I'm not asking for your approval. I just want to continue to be part of our family. I love all of you very much and I don't see why my being gay should change how you feel about me."

It Takes Time for Attitudes to Change

If your parents or other family members have a difficult time accepting the fact that you are a homosexual, remain patient and understanding of their feelings and attitudes. One would hope that with more time, tolerance, and communication they will accept you again as their son or daughter without your sexuality being an issue.

#91 "WE WANT TO PUT YOU IN A RETIREMENT HOME."

Is your elder parent increasingly absentminded and confused? Does he or she forget to take medication, not eat regularly, or need daily care? Suggesting that a parent with diminished mental or physical capabilities get assistance or move into a retirement home may prove to be a difficult, yet necessary conversation. Experts in the field of elder care offer the following strategies for adult children who plan to provide additional care for their parents.

Before you open the discussion with your parent, do your homework. Determine what additional care your parent needs and find out what options are available. Some possibilities include visits from home-care workers, moving into a retirement community, or, in extreme cases, receiving continuous medical care in a nursing home. Never make a decision about a retirement or nursing home without first visiting the facility or meeting the director.

Whenever possible, discuss the need for care with your parent so that he or she recognizes the reality of the situation. If your parent denies needing help, remind him or her of recent situations that bring into focus the seriousness of the problem. For example, you can say:

"Dad, remember last week, you fell and burned your hand on the stove? You don't have any food in the refrigerator except what we brought you, and the trash hasn't been taken out in at least a week. I think it is pretty clear that if someone came in five days a week to help you, it would make things a lot easier for you. Do you agree?"

If your parent denies the need for help or placement in a retirement home, then ask your parent's doctor to make a specific recommendation. Focus on the benefits of additional care in terms of safety, happiness, peace of mind, and improved quality of life.

Here's what you can say:

"Mom, I'm concerned about your safety and well-being and so is your doctor. We're afraid that you're not eating properly or taking your medicine every day. When was the last

time you saw any of your friends? Dr. Jones asked that you consider moving into a retirement community where you have your own apartment, proper meals, and medical care. Plus, think of all the new friends you'll make!"

Whenever possible, allow your parent to be part of the planning process. Visit prospective facilities first without your parent to see what the staff and accommodations are like. First explain the benefits of living in such a place in terms of how they will *help* you and your parent.

For example, you can say:

"I went to visit Hillview Senior Citizens Community yesterday, and was I impressed! You don't have to worry about preparing your own meals or shopping, and there are plenty of social activities. Think of all the fun you can be having when you are around more people. Plus, I'll have peace of mind knowing that your basic living needs are taken care of."

Then describe the specific features the facility offers, such as food, staff, activities, and accommodations. You might say something like:

"You should see the cafeteria menus! It's like a four-star restaurant! There are friendly doctors, nurses, recreation directors, and other staff whenever you need them. Plus, I can't wait to show you the apartments, swimming pool, hot tub, game room, and all the other facilities. I think you're going to really like this place."

Plan a visit together to let your parent form his or her own opinion. Then, if possible, reach a consensus and joint decision. You can say:

"Well, what do you think? Could you be happy in a nice place of your own where everything is taken care of for you? Did you like the people there? Are you willing to give it a try?"

If your parent isn't sure about making the move, he or she may be concerned about the financial arrangements or some other details. Encourage him or her to open up by saying:

"You seem hesitant about something. What is it? Tell me what's on your mind so that we can talk about it."

If your parent says:

"How much is all this going to cost? I'm worried about the money."

You can respond:

"I've listed all the expenses and we can talk about how to cover the costs. Look, Dad, nothing is cast in stone. If you don't like it, we'll work something else out, but for now I think this is your best bet. How about it?"

DOS AND DON'TS WHEN TALKING TO YOUR PARENTS

Do talk to your parents with respect.

Don't assume that you and your parents share the same values.

Do make an effort to seek their advice and counsel.

Don't expect your parents to rescue you from a bad situation.

Do show your appreciation for what your parents do for you.

Don't contrast your parents with your friends' parents.

Do accept your parents for who they are and make an effort to get along.

Don't focus on events from the distant past that made you angry at your parents.

Do forgive your parents for their child-rearing mistakes.

Don't let your parents' fears or overcritical views paralyze your efforts to achieve your dreams.

CHAPTER 15

Tactful Ways to Tell Your Relatives . . .

Do your relatives drive you up the wall with their tacky remarks, pushy opinions, sarcastic comments, or nosy questions? Are you so competitive with a brother or sister that it strains your relationship? Do your in-laws pressure you into doing things that you'd rather avoid? Are there times when you need to inform your relatives of a personal decision of which they will disapprove?

There's no question about it that while most of your relatives are probably as lovable as pussycats, coping with the annoying members of your family is truly challenging! Even so, by talking with tact you can take the wind out of their sails and do what you want—without their interference.

#92 "MIND YOUR OWN BUSINESS!"

There are many situations where you may feel like telling your pushy relatives to stay out of your business. For the sake of family peace, however, you must tactfully deflect unwelcome comments and suggestions from relatives who are Steamrollers, Know-It-Alls, Bushwhackers, and Wet Blankets. When you stand up to these rascals, you not only earn their respect and build your self-esteem, you get them to leave you alone!

For example, if your nosy sister-in-law asks how much money you make, you can say something like:

"Well, business has been pretty good this year. I can't give you an exact figure, but we're doing fine. Why do you ask?"

If she says:

"Well . . . I was wondering if it might be a profession I could get into, but I'd want to know how much I could make before getting too involved. So . . . how much do you make?"

You can respond:

"It's a rather personal question, you know. But if you are thinking about making a career change, why not come down to our office some afternoon and I'll fill you in on more of the details?"

If your Steamroller mother-in-law tries to bully you into sending your child to an expensive private school instead of a public school by saying:

"I honestly don't know how any loving parent could ever even consider sending his or her child to a public school. Everyone knows the teachers are nothing but overpaid baby-sitters. Don't you think so?"

Take a deep breath. Then in a forceful but friendly manner say:

"Well, mother-in-law, I don't agree with you. As a matter of fact, I know several parents whose children attend our local elementary school and they are quite pleased with their children's progress. I visited the school, met the principal and several teachers, and I was quite impressed. But I'm curious how you came to have such a strong opinion about this issue in the first place."

If your Know-It-All brother tries to goad you into buying an expensive sports car by saying:

"No compact car for my brother-in-law! No, sir! What you need is something to bring out the man in you. It's a super-high-performance Corvette and it will only cost you one hundred and fifty-five dollars more per month than that ugly compact you want to buy."

You can calmly respond in a methodical manner by saying:

"If I understand you correctly, the sports car will cost me one hundred and fifty-five dollars a month more than the compact car. That doesn't sound like that much, but if it takes me five years to pay off the car loan, it would cost me over nine thousand dollars more to buy the sports car than the compact. Sorry, but that sports car is too rich for my blood! But I'd love to borrow your Corvette when you can afford to buy one!"

If your Wet Blanket cousin throws water on your goal of going back to school by saying:

"You want to go back to school and become a lawyer? You'll be in a class full of kids and they'll be calling you grandpa!"

You can acknowledge the Wet Blanket's point and ask for help by saying:

"You might be right. It could take me some time to adjust, but so what? I want to get a good-paying job and I think this is the way to get it. Say, isn't your neighbor a lawyer? Do you think he might be willing to give me some advice on where to go to school?"

#93 "STOP MAKING NASTY COMMENTS ABOUT MY SPOUSE!"

Do your relatives make nasty remarks behind your spouse's back? Do they constantly needle you about his or her shortcomings? When your relatives do talk face-to-face with your spouse, are they sarcastic or condescending? If you want to stop their outward negativity toward your spouse, then you must speak up, but do it in a tactful way.

Use a strategy of standing up for yourself and your spouse by gently confronting the disapproving relative without arguing. If you make it clear that you don't like what he or she is saying and you want the nasty comments to stop, he or she will probably back off—at least for a while. Here are some examples of what you can say to get backbiting relatives to stop maligning your spouse.

If your busybody relative says:

"If you want my opinion, you should have married. . . . You'd have been much happier and richer!"

Respond in a firm, strong voice using any of the following examples:

"Hold it, Aunt Mabel. First of all, I'm happily married. And second, I didn't ask your opinion. I don't like it when I hear you making nasty comments about my spouse. But if something about my husband is bothering you, why don't you just come right out and say it."

"It upsets me when I hear you make sarcastic remarks about my spouse. I know you said that you were just kidding, but to me your comments just sound like you want our marriage to fail. Did you mean them to sound that way?"

"I don't appreciate you running down my spouse like that. It's really bad manners and I'd like you to stop."

"You may not approve of the way we live—you're entitled to your opinion—but we are entitled to live the way we choose. I think it would be best if you'd keep your opinions to yourself."

"If you've got a problem with my spouse, why don't you bring it up with him directly instead of grumbling behind his back?"

#94 "THIS GIFT IS TRULY AWFUL!"

Wouldn't it be great if you loved every gift from your relatives? However, this is wishful thinking! Suppose your aunt gives you an extra-large punch bowl when what you really need is a small frying pan. Your brother-in-law gives you a pipe and you've just quit smoking. Your sister insists on buying you clothes that look better on her than they do on you. Your cousin gives you a driftwood lamp covered with seashells that he made at summer camp! The list of useless, ugly, and tasteless gifts goes on and on!

The tactful response to a disappointing gift is first to show surprise, then fake—yes, fake—delight. Finally, of course, say, ***"Thank you."***

Here are some ways to show a somewhat cool response without coming right out and saying that you are disappointed with the gift.

You can say:

"What a nice gift! Thank you!"

"Thank you! This really is an interesting gift. What is it exactly?"

"Oh, thank you! I've never seen anything like this before! Oh, you made it? You're so handy!"

Quietly accepting an unwanted present also has its hazards. Since your aunt assumes that you like her hand-painted plaster statue, don't be surprised when you get another one next year. However, if you choose to give the gift away, have an excuse ready if your aunt drops by and doesn't see her handiwork adorning your living room coffee table.

A more frequent problem is how to tell a relative that you'd like to exchange a gift. When you face this delicate situation, take the gift-giving relative aside and gently say something like:

"I love the color of this sweater, but it just doesn't seem to fit me quite right. If you tell me where you got it, I'd like to exchange it for one that fits me a bit better, if that's okay."

"I think the platter you gave me is quite beautiful, but I've got a bit of a problem. I simply don't have any room to store it and I don't entertain such large groups anymore. Would you be very hurt if I exchanged it for a smaller size? I don't

mind taking care of the exchange if you tell me where you
bought it."

Now, if you really don't care for the item, you can always say
that you couldn't find a suitable replacement, and you exchanged it for something else that was just perfect.

#95 "I DON'T WANT TO COMPETE WITH YOU ANYMORE."

"Mom always liked you best!" Sibling rivalry that began in child-
hood often continues well into adulthood. Do you have a competitive relationship with a brother or a sister? Is the rivalry
between you friendly enough on the surface but actually more
serious than either of you cares to admit? Is your rivalry hurting
other members of your family by making them choose sides?

Breaking a lifelong competition with a sibling is a challenge.
Admitting the harm of unhealthy competition and confronting
the issue helps bring the problem out into the open. Then each
of you must redefine your individual roles and how you relate
to each other. Here are some ways to reveal your concern that
the competition between you and a sibling has gone too far.

You can say:

> *"I'm worried that what used to be friendly competition be-
> tween you and me has gotten way out of hand. As far as I'm
> concerned, I think arguing about who went to the better
> school, who makes the most money, or who has the most
> expensive car hurts our relationship."*

If your sibling says in a challenging voice:

> *"Giving up? I guess you've finally figured out that I'm bet-
> ter than you, right?"*

You can respond without malice:

> *"Maybe you're right. I think both of us have been taking
> this competition thing too seriously for too long. Let's cool
> it, okay?"*

If your sibling tries to entice you into a verbal match by saying:

> *"What's wrong? Are you too old and tired to take me on? Are you finally giving up?"*

You can ignore the challenge and calmly respond:

> *"Look, competing with each other was fun when we were kids. It was motivating then, but I don't think either of us needs to do that now. We're both good at what we do, so why not just leave it at that? Anyway I feel it is much healthier to compete against my business rivals than against my own brother (or sister)."*

If your sibling boasts of extravagant accomplishments or belittles your recent achievements with the hope of drawing you into a competitive exchange, don't respond to the challenge. Instead acknowledge his or her worth as an individual. For example, you can say something like:

> *"I think it's great that you can buy a house on the beach and one in the mountains too. I'm glad you're doing so well and I hope it continues. You deserve it. But your successes have nothing to do with me."*

If you back off from the competition with your sibling, then he or she will have to look for someone else to compete with. Since these patterns go back a long way, don't be surprised if you continue to hear familiar jabs. You can respond to these recurring challenges by saying:

> *"I read about two brothers who live in the same neighborhood but haven't spoken to each other for over ten years just because they couldn't stop competing with each other! Even when they saw each other at their father's funeral, they wouldn't exchange words. I never want that to happen with us, so please do us both a big favor—find someone else to compete with."*

#96 "YOU CAN'T STAY HERE!"

Do some of your relatives assume that you are delighted to provide them with room and board when they visit you? It might surprise you, but many people unwittingly ask for unwanted houseguests by offering open invitations to relatives—especially at family gatherings. One way to minimize the number of relatives who ask for your hospitality is to NEVER say:

"Drop by and visit if you're passing through our area."

"We'd love to show off our wonderful city."

"We just finished painting our guest room."

"Hotels are so expensive nowadays! That's why we bought a camper that comfortably sleeps five."

If your better judgment slipped and you suggested at the family reunion that everyone come and visit, be prepared for telephone calls from distant or unwanted relatives that sound something like this:

"Remember at last year's family reunion when you said if we were ever in the area to stop by? Well, my wife and three kids will be in your town next week and we were wondering if we could stay with you for a few days."

So, how do you hang out the No Vacancy sign to unwanted visitors? Even if you offered your hospitality, you can tactfully retract the invitation by using any of these apologies, excuses, or "little white lies."

Here are several examples of how tactfully to take back your hospitality:

"Did I say that? It was so long ago. I'm sorry, but we have plans for that weekend. Do you want the name of a local hotel? I hope we get to see you at least for a short time while you're in town."

"What bad timing. Next weekend is really not a good time for us. We'll be out of town."

"What a shame. We already have a houseful of guests for that weekend."

"I'm sorry, but that whole month is totally impossible. I'm overloaded with work and I can't possibly entertain guests."

"We're in the middle of a renovation, so we don't have any room."

If your relatives say:

"Oh, we won't bother you. We don't need anything fancy. We'll be as quiet as church mice."

You can say:

"I'm sure you wouldn't be any trouble, but as I said before, that is really an inconvenient time for us to have guests. If you'd like, I'd be happy to make reservations at one of our local hotels. What's in your budget?"

#97 "PLEASE LEAVE TOMORROW."

If you are willing to put up with relatives as houseguests, you can save yourself stress, embarrassment, and inconvenience if you explain certain "house rules" to them from the beginning. For example, you are certainly entitled to ask:

"When are you coming and how long do you think you want to stay?"

The key is to limit the length of your guest's stay by saying something like:

"You're welcome to stay with us through Wednesday, but after that I'm afraid you'll have to be on your own."

"If you're looking for a place to stay a little longer, we do have some nice motels in our area. You might want to take a look around and see what you can find that is within your budget."

Tell your relatives in a friendly way that you have certain expectations as far as their visit with you is concerned. With a pleasant smile you can lay out house rules by saying:

"Please do me a favor and pick up after yourselves."

"Do you like to cook? Feel free to use the kitchen, but please clean up after yourself."

"By the way, there's a grocery store on the corner where you can buy milk, coffee, bread, eggs, or whatever you want to eat."

"Also, I hope you don't mind not smoking in the house, because I'm terribly allergic to smoke."

HOW TO ASK A GUEST TO LEAVE

If the visit begins to extend past your limits of hospitality, then you will need to tell your guests tactfully but firmly to leave. Take your relative by the arm and, with a warm smile, suggest that you are ready to say good-bye and have your home back to yourself. You can drop the hint if you say:

"It's been wonderful that you've come to visit, and I hope you've enjoyed your stay. I only wish we had more time to spend together, but I've got so many things to do around here—such as painting our guest room. Where are you off to next in your travels?"

If you've reached your limit, but your relative fails to pick up the hint that it's time to go, then just be direct and don't worry about insulting him or her. After all, it is your house, and what is more offensive than a sponging relative who outstays his or her welcome? Here's what you can say:

"I've enjoyed visiting with you and hearing all about the family, but quite honestly I need my privacy back. It's nothing personal, but let's make tonight your last one for this visit."

#98 "NO, I CAN'T HELP YOU."

Relatives love to ask for unreasonable favors. These favors take a variety of forms, but they can all be dealt with in essentially the same way—an assertive *no*.

Saying too much is the mistake that many people make. Even if you feel guilty about saying *no*, don't concoct elaborate excuses. Chances are, you'll get so caught up in your own lies that to avoid total embarrassment, you'll give in to the most imposing request. An effective strategy is to deny the request politely by saying:

"As much as I would like to, I just couldn't. . . ."

Then shut up, no matter how long a period of silence follows! Each time your persistent relative asks for the favor in another way, use the "broken record" assertive technique described in Chapter 4. Here are some typical favors that your relatives may ask and assertive ways to give a polite refusal.

If your relative asks:

"Can you loan me five hundred dollars? I'll pay you back as soon as I get paid, I promise."

You can say:

"I'd like to be able to help you out, but it just isn't possible."

If your relative tries to push it by asking:

"Why not? You've got a good job and plenty of money."

You can say:

"We must not be talking to the same banker! I'm sorry, but it's impossible for me to do that."

If the relative asks:

"Can our two teenagers stay with you for the summer while we travel in Europe?"

You can say:

"That wouldn't be possible. No, I don't believe we could. Sorry."

If they try to pressure you by saying:

"Why not? Our kids wouldn't be any trouble. They're angels, I promise."

You can say:

"I'm sure your kids would be perfect houseguests, but I'm afraid I can't help you out. We already have plans for the summer."

If a relative asks:

"You're a carpenter and I need a new bedroom. How about you building it for me and we'll work something out?"

You can say:

"I'd love to be able to help you, but I'm afraid I'll have to decline. I'm really sorry, but I can't."

If the relative pressures you by asking:

"It won't be that much work. Come on, what's the big deal? We're family, aren't we?"

You can say:

"Of course we're family, and that's only one reason why I'm not going to get involved in a project that I couldn't possibly finish to your satisfaction. Sorry, but you'd be far better off getting a contractor to do the kind of job you're talking about. Let me give you the telephone number of someone who might be interested in the job."

If your sweet-talking brother-in-law asks:

"Can you help my buddy out of his tax mess? He really needs a break."

You can say:

"I'd like to, but there's no way I can take on any new clients right now. I'm up to my eyeballs in work right now."

If your relative tries to pressure you by saying:

"Hey, you're making me look like a liar. I told him you were a hot-shot tax lawyer and a really nice guy. Come on, won't you help him, please?"

You can say:

"It's impossible for me to get involved. If you want, I can give you the name of an accountant who might be able to help, but he won't do it for free."

HOW TO USE A STALLING TACTIC

When people are surprised or caught off guard by a request, they often find themselves agreeing to do things they'd rather not. If your relative tries to make you feel guilty and butters you up with compliments, use this stalling tactic until you can muster your strength to say *no* and mean it. Here are several examples of ways you can postpone your answer:

"Gee, I really couldn't tell you right now. I'll have to let you know tomorrow."

"Let me check with my husband (wife, boss, partner, etc.) and get back to you on that."

"I couldn't possibly answer that right now. I'll call you later."

"I don't think I'm free that weekend. I'll call you back later when I can look at my calendar."

Remember, you do not have to give a specific reason why you are declining the request. If necessary, script what you want to say and practice before you speak to the other person.

You can say something like:

"I'd love to be able to help you, but it's just not possible."

"I wish you all the success, but you'll have to do it without me."

"I'd like to be able to help you move, but my doctor said not to lift anything heavy."

"I'm afraid I can't be of any help."

"I'd love to, but I've made other plans."

"Sorry, I'm afraid I have to say no."

#99 "OUR KID IS ON DRUGS."

It is embarrassing for parents to admit to other family members that their teenager has a drug problem. Some naive relatives may deny that a problem exists or disagree with your plans to seek professional help. Self-righteous relatives may blame you for setting a poor example, being too lenient, or failing to see the signs of drug abuse before now. Here are some ways to tell relatives about your child's drug-abuse problem and what you are doing about it.

You can say in a straightforward way:

"Grandpa, Pat has been coming home a lot with the smell of liquor on his breath. At first we didn't want to make a big deal about it, but then we got a call from school about him missing classes and his slipping grades. We talked to him, but it didn't do any good. Last week he got arrested for underage drinking. We went to a doctor, who recommended that Pat attend a substance-abuse treatment program. All of us are attending family education and therapy sessions, which of course you are invited to join."

If the relative says:

"An alcohol treatment program for my grandson? You're nuts! Pat is just a typical teenage boy who likes to have a good time and drink a little. Why, I started drinking when I was a teenager and it hasn't done me any harm. Let me talk to him, and I'll straighten everything out."

You can respond:

"We appreciate your offer to help, but Pat is abusing alcohol and other drugs, and the sooner we get professional help for him, the better. These kinds of problems just don't go away by themselves. The rehabilitation counselors told us that the greater the family involvement, the sooner Pat will learn to face his problems without booze or drugs."

If another critical relative says:

"You should have sent him to a military academy like I suggested and this never would have happened. You should throw the kid out of the house until he cleans up his act!"

You can hold your ground, remain cool, and say:

"Maybe you're right about the academy, but I disagree with you about abandoning Pat to the streets. Alcohol and drug addiction are illnesses that can be treated professionally, and we are going to stand behind our son and get him the help he needs."

#100 "YOU'RE EMBARRASSING THE WHOLE FAMILY."

It seems that family get-togethers always bring out the most annoying habits in relatives. For example, does your thrifty grandfather insist on prying free medical advice from a guest who happens to be a physician? Does your undependable brother always arrive late and then drink too much? Does your sister-in-law argue with anyone who does not share her political views?

This is your family, so go easy—that is, unless an unmanageable relative is causing you or someone else in your family a particular problem. If that is the case, you may want to step in to say a few well-chosen words. If at all possible, take your rude relative aside and speak to him or her in private. Keep your cool, don't start scolding or preaching, but instead use a light touch and humor to get your point across. Here are some typical embarrassing comments from relatives and how to handle them.

When your frugal relative says:

"Why shouldn't I ask my son-in-law to look at my teeth? He's a dentist, isn't he? After all, we are feeding him dinner, aren't we?"

You can say:

"Yes, he is a dentist and yes he is eating dinner here because we invited him as a guest! If you want to get your teeth examined, why don't you call his office and get an appointment? I'm sure he'd be happy to look over your choppers."

When your drunk cousin says:

"Oh, come on, one more little drink for the road."

You can say:

"Sorry, but you've had quite enough to drink. If you have any more, I'm going to have to get a wheelbarrow to carry you out of here. In fact, I'm going to ask Uncle Phil to give

*you a ride home, because you're in no condition to drive.
Good night!"*

When your belligerent uncle attacks your brother by saying:

*"Anyone who thinks like you do ought to be strung up and
quartered. It's people like you who are causing our country
to go down the drain!"*

You can say:

*"Well, it's pretty clear that the two of you are not going to
agree on any political issues, so why don't you just drop it
before World War III breaks out? Uncle Carl, why don't
you tell the rest of us about your last vacation in Europe?"*

Keep in mind that in most cases rude relatives will take a reprimand for the moment, but the next time your family meets,
don't be surprised when they go back to their old tricks!

#101 "LET'S STOP THIS FEUDING ONCE AND FOR ALL."

Do you have a long-standing feud with a member of your family? Did something happen between the two of you long ago that
made one or both of you so angry that you no longer talk to
each other? Are other members of your family upset by this rift
and frustrated because they are often asked to serve as go-
betweens? Has the hostility between you reached the point
where neither of you can be in the same room without bombarding each other with accusations?

The old saying "Time heals all wounds" certainly does not
always apply to family feuds. In fact the passage of time tends to
exaggerate the conflict out of proportion. Personal feuds between relations are as destructive to the other members of the
family as they are to the warring participants, but the bottom
line is that when relatives fight, everyone in the family suffers.

TAKING THE FIRST STEP

It takes guts to be the one who takes the initiative to end a family
feud. To help you overcome the fear of rejection and failure,
ask yourself the following questions:

"What do I have to lose by trying to end this feud?"

"What do I have to gain if this feud ends?"

"What does my family have to lose by me trying to end this feud?"

"What does my family have to gain if this feud ends?"

Here are other reasons for taking the first step to end the feud:

- The other person may be waiting for you to make the first move.
- It shows that you are no longer angry at the other person.
- You are willing to admit your own mistakes and responsibility in the conflict.
- You've reconsidered the priority of the conflict and you feel it is no longer important enough to divide your family.
- You feel that relieving your family's anguish is more important than personal pride or who was right or wrong.
- You believe that your family's unity is more important than anything else and that it benefits all its members.

BE PATIENT AND THOUGHTFUL ABOUT THE HEALING PROCESS

Reestablishing the communication links between angry family members takes time, good timing, patience, and strategic planning and is most fruitful when executed in small steps with reasonable expectations. You can make a "peace offering" or apologize to a relative with whom you are fighting in person, by telephone, by letter, or through a third party.

IT'S NEVER TOO LATE TO APOLOGIZE FOR A MISTAKE

The intended impact of an apology is to dissolve another's anger for the purpose of forgiveness and reconciliation. Here is what you can say:

"That was such a crazy time in my life, and I did several regrettable things that hurt the people that mattered to me

the most. I don't blame you one bit for being angry with me. I'm sorry I spoke to you that way and I hope that you can forgive me."

"I'm sorry for what I did to you and I'm sure you'll never forget it. I just hope you can forgive me so that we can stop this constant fighting over what happened so many years ago."

"I realize that after all this time I'm not angry at you anymore and that I have to shoulder some of the blame for us not getting along. I accept that we don't always have to agree on things. I'm sorry that I said those hurtful words to you and I hope you can forgive me. For the sake of everyone in the family, can we at least be on speaking terms again? I miss you!"

"I owe you an apology. I'm sorry I lost my temper, but it was a long time ago. I want to forgive and forget. Are you ready to become friends again?"

REESTABLISH YOUR RELATIONSHIP ONE STEP AT A TIME

It takes time to get a damaged relationship back to where it was before the feud erupted. Take it slow and let the trust build naturally. There may be a time when the two of you can discuss what went wrong without feeling defensive or getting upset. Or, you may never talk about the issue that divided you. The point at which a feud finally ends is up to the relatives involved, but everyone will benefit and rejoice when the people in your family get back together.

Conclusion

The strategies, skills, and suggestions presented in this book work, but only if *you* use them and adapt them to your own situations. You've learned how to think before you speak, listen effectively, relax under pressure, assert yourself, and cope with troublesome personalities. With 101 difficult situations and hundreds of examples as a guide, you are ready to tactfully communicate your thoughts and feelings at work and at home.

Imagine the confidence you'll feel as you openly discuss delicate subjects without making others feel embarrassed, offended, or defensive. People will respond in a way that may surprise you when you talk to them tactfully—they'll like and respect you! What more could you ask for?

About the Author

Don Gabor, author and interpersonal communications skills trainer, is the "small talk" expert. He has been writing and speaking about the art of conversation since 1980 and presents seminars to businesses, corporations, associations, nonprofit organizations, universities, and schools. He is a member of the National Speakers Association and the American Society for Training and Development.

Don Gabor is dedicated to helping people of all ages achieve success and build their self-esteem, confidence, and leadership potential through better interpersonal communication. He founded Conversation Arts Media in 1991 to realize this goal.

To find out how you can arrange for Don Gabor to speak before your group or how to obtain his books, audiocassettes, videos, booklets, and a free conversation tip sheet, "50 Ways to Improve Your Conversations," please contact:

Don Gabor
Conversation Arts Media
P.O. Box 150-715
Brooklyn, NY 11215-0008

Telephone: 718-768-0824